D0874019

Praise for *Diversity and Inclusion Matters*

"As a Diversity Officer, implementing DE&I programs can be challenging. Having known Jason and worked with him, his insight and knowledge on DE&I will provide CEOs an understanding of how they can lead and support DE&I initiatives impactfully. This is a must-read for all working in the professional world."

—**Dominic F. Martinez, EdD,** Assistant Vice Chancellor, Office of Inclusion and Outreach, Undocumented Student Services; Assistant Professor, Department of Family Medicine, University of Colorado Anschutz Medical Campus

"Since I have known Jason, diversity and inclusion have always been of utmost importance to him in every professional leadership role he has held. This book is only an extension of him making those important lessons of how to shift your organization through diversity and inclusion accessible to everyone."

—**Kimberly Morgan,** DE&I Sr. Director, GOJO Industries

"I first met Jason when our company hired him to develop and implement a DE&I program. His expertise, coupled with clear and practical advice, was instrumental in the development of our program. *Diversity and Inclusion Matters* is a much-needed roadmap for any corporation looking to implement a state-of-the-art DE&I program."

—**Beth Pauchnik, RN, JD,** Senior Healthcare Executive

"Jason's approach to activating DE&I within an organization is spot on. In *Diversity and Inclusion Matters* he outlines concise and clear guidelines on how to implement DE&I and maintain and create transformational change. As an entrepreneur with a longtime career in team management and organizational development, I highly recommend this for any leader who wants to really embed DE&I into the DNA of their organizations."

—**Andrea Perdomo,** Director, Economic Inequality Initiative, Uncharted

"As we all know, DE&I has been at the forefront of business as a differentiator, and yet there are almost no practical, real-world examples of *how* to implement an effective program. I liked the way Jason approached trying to change the organization culture by attending and speaking at comparable sporting organizations such as PGA, MLB, and the NFL."

—**John (JR) Register,** Mindsight Warrior;
Paralympic Silver Medalist

"I met Jason early on in my pharmacy career in 2003, and to this day, the positive impact he had on me as a person and professional is everlasting. Jason was always a safe place to ask questions regarding my position and the expectations. Jason was committed to diversity and inclusion before it became a buzzword, and he represents a wealth of knowledge and experience."

—**Leticia (Tisha) Smith, PharmD, BCACP,**
Assistant Director of Ambulatory Clinical Pharmacy, Denver Health

"The continued drive towards DE&I in health care is an imperative to our success and future. Jason always impresses with his unique approach and practical applications. His insights allow you to tailor a DE&I program that aligns with your company's culture. This book is an excellent tool for your team!"

—**Avilla Williams,** Vice President Clinical Services,
Integris Health

DIVERSITY

AND

INCLUSION
MATTERS

TACTICS *and* TOOLS *to* INSPIRE
EQUITY *and* GAME-CHANGING
PERFORMANCE

JASON R. THOMPSON

WILEY

Published by John Wiley & Sons, Inc., Hoboken, New Jersey.
Published simultaneously in Canada.

For general information on our other products and services or for technical support, please contact our Customer Care Department within the United States at (800) 762–2974, outside the United States at (317) 572–3993, or fax (317) 572–4002.

Wiley publishes in a variety of print and electronic formats and by print-on-demand. Some material included with standard print versions of this book may not be included in e-books or in print-on-demand. If this book refers to media such as a CD or DVD that is not included in the version you purchased, you may download this material at http://booksupport.wiley.com. For more information about Wiley products, visit www.wiley.com.

Library of Congress Cataloging-in-Publication Data

Names: Thompson, Jason (Professor), author.
Title: Diversity and inclusion matters : tactics and tools to inspire
   equity and game-changing performance / Jason Thompson.
Description: Hoboken, NJ : Wiley, [2022] | Includes index.
Identifiers: LCCN 2021039751 (print) | LCCN 2021039752 (ebook) | ISBN
   9781119799535 (Hardback) | ISBN 9781119799559 (epdf) | ISBN
   9781119799542 (epub)
Subjects: LCSH: Diversity in the workplace. | Equality.
Classification: LCC HF5549.5.M5 T47 2022 (print) | LCC HF5549.5.M5
   (ebook) | DDC 331.13/3—dc23/eng/20211007
LC record available at https://lccn.loc.gov/2021039751
LC ebook record available at https://lccn.loc.gov/2021039752

COVER DESIGN: PAUL MCCARTHY
COVER ART: © JUSTUS THOMPSON

SKY10030233_110321

Contents

Preface

Telling Stories and Bridging the Disconnect

In order to make connections and foster understanding, we must cross bridges. Selma, Alabama, is the site of one of the most powerful bridge crossings in the history of the United States. On July 26, 2020, the body of civil rights leader and American statesmen John Robert Lewis was taken across Selma's Edmund Pettus Bridge one last time as his funeral procession made its way to the Alabama state capital. In 1965, Lewis had nearly lost his life during the Bloody Sunday march on that bridge, which peaceful Civil Rights demonstrators crossed in order to reach Alabama's state capital. In the decades that followed, Lewis worked tirelessly to make sure that bridge would remain open and crossable – both literally and figuratively – for everyone.

My work in diversity, equity, and inclusion (DE&I) in no way compares to Lewis's commitment or accomplishments, but I have endeavored to honor the importance of his historic crossing. I feel strongly that the more we can bridge the divides that separate us, the better we can make this world. As a DE&I professional, building bridges is fundamental to my work.

Over the last 25 years of working on DE&I programs for the US Olympic and Paralympic Committee (USOPC), major sports organizations, institutions of higher education, and large corporations, I have developed a reputation for telling stories that help people build and cross bridges. People often tell me they enjoy my simple stories, and some even go as far as to tell me I have a gift. If I have a gift, it is as a motivator to help people bridge divides, create new understandings, and collaborate – not *despite* their differences but *because* of their differences.

My Story

I was born in Japan on a military base to an African American father and a Japanese mother. I have no memories of Japan because after I was born we soon moved to Hawaii. We were a family of six, and I am the youngest of four children. After five years in Hawaii, my dad was transferred to the Air Force base in Cheyenne, Wyoming. I lived in Wyoming until I was in my late 20s.

Growing up in Wyoming was difficult because there are few people with brown skin. My family did not have much money, partly because my parents did not make a lot of money and partly because my dad always made bad decisions with the money we did have. I struggled in school, yet somehow, despite my dyslexia, I graduated from the University of Wyoming with both a bachelor's and a master's degree.

Probably even more unlikely, as a graduate student, I became the first Person of Color to be the student body president at the University of Wyoming. The election process was full of tension and heavy with undertones of racism. On the first day I put up my posters, I received a phone call from someone threatening to beat me up. In addition, it seemed as if my campaign posters were being ripped down within an hour of my putting them up. On a daily basis, students would say to me, "You need to put posters up, or people are not going to know you are running for student body president." What they did not know was I spent the first hour of every morning walking all over campus putting up posters only to have someone rip them down.

In what now seems like a scene from a story made for a movie, one of the two candidates I was running against wore a hat with the Confederate flag on it. To make the story even more outlandish, the advisor to the student government allowed the fraternity brothers of the incumbent student body president to count the votes for the primary election. The incumbent's fraternity brothers decided it was necessary to throw out ten votes, which meant that I came in ten votes behind the incumbent. Nonetheless, I still made it to the general election runoff against the incumbent.

As the general election drew nearer, things continued to become more contentious. I experienced threats of violence, and my campaign posters, which included a picture of my young son, were defaced with insults and put everywhere to make sure I saw them. The defaced posters were put on the door of the graduate student office I shared with other graduate students in the Sociology Department and on the door of the Multicultural Resource Center where I worked. My wife worked on campus at that time, and she, too, was threatened at work by students who supported the incumbent. The election became so charged with tension that the city of Laramie was asked to bring in their official election equipment, and the city employees conducted the voting process. This was the first and only time in the history of the University of Wyoming when a student election required the oversight of professional election staff and equipment.

In the end, the majority of students at the University of Wyoming saw the divide and crossed the bridge. I won by a landslide on a predominantly white campus with barely 100 Black students. My personal story is one of crossing bridges and overcoming obstacles.

The Bridge Between Intent and Impact

Every company, institution, organization, or association will, at some point either realize the benefits – economic, moral, and social – of diversity, equity, and inclusion, or, in spite of its blindness, will be forced to create programs to survive. There are a lot of DE&I programs, and even more are being started every day. Unfortunately, many of them struggle to fulfill their intentions, and they make common mistakes.

To help illustrate how difficult this process can be, I like to share a story from my personal life. I have dyslexia but was not diagnosed until adulthood. Growing up, I was often told that I was a terrible reader, but my teachers and parents didn't know that I was dyslexic – and I wasn't even aware such a condition existed. Because no one knew the root of my reading troubles, I was often told to work harder on becoming a better reader. To become a better reader, I needed a bridge. It wasn't just about working harder. Identifying a problem (I was a terrible reader) is different from diagnosing it (I am dyslexic), so simply working harder was never a solution. I have worked on being a better reader and writer, but the turning point was being able to type on a computer that can identify my mistakes in real time as I make them. For example, no matter how often I type my first name, I typically misspell it. Luckily, spellcheck puts a red line under my name whenever I make an error. The computer is a bridge to better reading and writing because it helps me see the errors and the solutions. Without that bridge, I simply could not see the errors I was making.

My daily misspellings are a reminder that disconnects can cause problems everywhere. When I cannot consistently spell my name correctly, despite all the repetition, it causes me to wonder whether the disconnect is in what I see or in something that got lost between my brain and hands. These personal challenges have made me think about DE&I differently. In my work, whenever I wonder *Why are so many DE&I programs struggling?* I know the real question is *Where is the disconnect?* To become a better reader, I had to identify the root of the problem. There is still some disconnect between my brain and hands, but there are tools that help me achieve. Similarly, trying to figure out where the disconnect is between intent and impact for diversity programs has driven me to find and create the tools to bridge the disconnect. For many diversity officers, there has been a gap between theory and execution, and the recommendations haven't worked.

This book was written to help diversity professionals, corporations, small businesses, large institutions, and associations cross the bridge from theory to execution. The message from the Ivory Tower is clear: We need bridges. But the high-level theory is less clear about where or how to build the bridges your organization needs. There are a lot of books and articles on the importance of DE&I and how it can make your organization more successful, yet companies have struggled to create diverse, equitable, and inclusive workspaces. They have not found the bridge.

Instead of theory, this book will give you time-tested tools and tried-and-true techniques to help you overcome the challenges of running DE&I programs. My coaching, advice, and techniques come from thousands of hours working with the US Olympic and Paralympic Committee, major sports organizations, large corporations, tech companies, universities, and countless DE&I professionals on what is needed to build successful DE&I programs. Throughout the book, you will also find *Jason-isms*. Jason-isms are things that people have pointed out that I say often to illustrate a point or concept.

I recently received a copy of a book on DE&I, and after reading it, I realized everything was theory. Nothing was practical. I then looked at the author's work experience and saw that the author had never actually ever worked as a DE&I professional in any capacity. Everything in the book was summarizing other articles, but there were no actual practical examples. Like most books and articles in this space, it explained the goal but not how to get there. The resources were good, but they lacked a practical application. As a result, I have gotten regular calls from seasoned professionals, as well as individuals new to working in the DE&I space, asking me for advice and recommendations.

That is why I decided to write this book. I have taken what I learned over 25 years of working in the DE&I space in four different industries to create practical tools and offer tips for creating DE&I programs. For example, it has been well documented that DE&I programs need CEO commitment, but what does that look like? What does the CEO *do* to show commitment? When does this happen? How can you measure it? I will give you practical advice and tips in this book to answer questions like this and many others that are about the day-to-day tasks that DE&I leaders need to execute to be successful.

My experience and approach have evolved to become a process I call CAPE. Each letter stands for a step you need to build a DE&I program:

C – Collect: Collect the necessary data.
A – Analyze: Review the data to identify the problem.
P – Plan: Create a plan to address the problem.
E – Execute: Progress toward meeting your goals and execute on your vision.

CAPE was specifically developed for solving DE&I problems, and it allows you to build the bridge to the right programs and measure the return on investment (ROI).

How the CAPE Process Works

In 2016 the Diversity Scorecard I developed for the US Olympic team was recognized as the number-one innovation in diversity by the *Profiles in Diversity Journal*.[1] With a budget of less than $60,000, I beat out companies like HP Inc., Cisco, Electronic Arts, and KPMG. I also received the Diversity Champion Award from the Colorado chapter of the Society for Human Resource Management (COSHRM), and I was twice named a Diversity Leader by Profiles in Diversity Journal.[2] I have been quoted in the *New York Times*,[3] the *Washington Post*,[4] the *Guardian*,[5] *USA Today*,[6] FOX News,[7] and CNN.[8]

Even before I had recognized it as a formalized process, I was using the CAPE principles to design award-winning DE&I programs. Now that the CAPE process is fully developed, this book will guide you through best practices and techniques that are very important but rarely explained. An article in *Fortune* titled "Chief Diversity Officers Are Set Up to Fail"[9] identified four major issues facing chief diversity officers:

1. They are new to the role.
2. They don't have the power they need to make a difference.
3. They don't have the data they need to make a difference.
4. Other leaders aren't on board.

In this book, you will learn first how to use the CAPE process to overcome these four challenges as well as others I have identified through my work with a range of organizations. Then, you'll learn more specific recommendations based on practical DE&I experiences that I've had with clients. To show you how DE&I looks in practice, I provide examples and solutions. For example, I will teach you how to set appropriate expectations for a DE&I program with the CEO and the executive leadership team. Unrealistic expectations are one of the biggest challenges for DE&I programs and chief diversity officers. You will benefit from my failures and successes.

Let's begin this journey together, and let me help you build your own bridges for DE&I.

Notes

1. On December 22, 2016, *Profiles in Diversity Journal* ran a headline naming the US Olympic Committee (USOC) and its D&I Scorecard as the number one innovation in diversity. Now an annual feature of the journal, the scorecard innovation was the brainchild of Jason Thompson who was the director of diversity and inclusion for the USOC. Accessed on April 5, 2021 at https://diversityjournal.com/16620-u-s-olympic-committee-di-scorecard-program/.
2. On March 8, 2018, Jason Thompson was given the Diversity Leader Award by the *Profiles in Diversity Journal* for over a decade's work and a series of accomplishments with the USOC including the QUAD hiring program, and the FLAME pipeline development program. Accessed on April 5, 2021 at https://diversityjournal.com/17083-jason-thompson-united-states-olympic-committee-2/.
3. On February 12, 2018, Jason Thompson was interviewed by and quoted in a *New York Times* article about diversity at the Winter Olympic Games in Pyeongchang, South Korea. Read the article: Talya

Minsberg, "A diverse Winter Olympics: but on the ground?" *New York Times*, February 12, 2018. Accessed on April 5, 2021 at https://www.nytimes.com/2018/02/12/sports/olympics/olympics-diversity-Maame-Biney-Fenlator-Victorian-Adigun.html.

4. Jason Thompson was interviewed by and quoted in a *Washington Post* article about diversity on the US Olympic Team going to the Winter Games in PyeongChang, South Korea. Read the article: Rick Maese, "Trying to make team USA look more like America,". *Washington Post*, February 4, 2018. Accessed on April 5, 2021 at https://www.washingtonpost.com/sports/olympics/trying-to-make-team-usa-look-more-like-america/2018/02/02/422ca13a-04fe-11e8–8777–2a059f168dd2_story.html.

5. In February 2018, Jason Thompson was quoted in the *Guardian* in an article about the diversity in the Winter Olympic Games in PyeongChang, South Korea. Read the article: Benjamin Haas, "Meet the Winter Olympians making big strides for diversity," The *Guardian*, February 16, 2018. Accessed on April 5, 2021 at https://www.theguardian.com/sport/2018/feb/17/winter-olympians-diversity-simidele-adeagbo-jazmine-fenlator-victorian.

6. *USA Today* quotes Jason Thompson in its article about diversity on the US Winter Olympics team. Read the article: Martin Rogers, "United States seeing uptick in diversity for Winter Olympics team," *USA Today*, February 5, 2018. Accessed on April 5, 2021 at https://www.usatoday.com/story/sports/winter-olympics-2018/2018/02/05/united-states-seeing-uptick-diversity-winter-olympics-team/308775002/.

7. A Fox News executive's comments about diversity on the US Olympic Team are called an embarrassment, and Jason Thompson's quotes from the *Washington Post* interview are explained and clarified. Read the article: Evan Grossman, "Fox News exec an American embarrassment for ripping idea of a more diverse Team USA at Winter Olympics," *New York Daily News*, February 10, 2018. Accessed on April 5, 2021 at https://www.nydailynews.com/sports/more-sports/fox-news-exec-embarrassment-ripping-diverse-team-usa-article-1.3810206.

8. CNN's Anderson Cooper quotes Jason Thompson in his Ridicu-List while blasting the Fox News exec who criticized USOC diversity initiatives. Watch the video here. Accessed on April 5, 2021 at https://www.cnn.com/videos/politics/2018/02/13/olympics-john-moody-fox-news-ridiculist-sot.cnn.

9. In March 2019 Ellen McGirt wrote a piece in *Fortune* magazine that highlighted four reasons why diversity officers were set up for failure, including the newness of the role, the lack of power, data, and CEO support. Read the article: Ellen McGirt, "Chief Diversity Officers are set up to fail," *Fortune*, March 4, 2019. Accessed on April 5, 2021 at https://fortune.com/2019/03/04/chief-diversity-officers-are-set-up-to-fail/.

Foreword

Dear Reader:

Covid-19. Amy Cooper. George Floyd. Police brutality. Black Lives Matter. The presidential election. The Capitol Riots. Social justice, systemic racism, equity – these are buzzwords from the past taking on new meaning, emphasis, importance, and scorn for a broader array of people. The United States is stepping into the global spotlight once again while casting a shadow that did not, and will not, serve its legacy well. Diversity and inclusion, for the first time, is becoming one of the most coveted roles in domestic and international corporations. The years 2020–2021 are years that have and continue to redefine how we view the world, how we view our neighbors, and how to have long overdue conversations within our communities and with corporations and governments. A roadmap for these conversations has never been more necessary or critical for the next generation.

A roadmap created and generously shared by my friend and colleague Jason R. Thompson is what you have here. Jason and I met through our mutual love of sports, he at the United States Olympic Committee and I through Major League Baseball (MLB). After many iterations of practicing law, I had the good fortune of securing my first diversity and inclusion role at the United States Tennis Association (USTA) and have not looked back in eleven years. It was a discipline I was not particularly familiar with, especially in professional spaces (my entry point thoroughly predates the current norm of DE&I practitioners at every law firm and government agency). But once exposed, I quickly realized I was more than ready for this work and that, in essence, I had been a DE&I champion my entire professional and personal life. My USTA experience exposed me to the nuances of a corporate America with the layer of a nonprofit entity. It was a unique and serendipitous starting point to say the least, and it prompted me to go further by gaining experience in other industries that offered a global lens to the agenda. This led to my pivot into DE&I roles at some incredible brands across several industries that prepared me for leadership roles at companies such as Gucci, Major League Baseball, and Harry's. In addition, I lead a DE&I consultancy through my company VegaRobles Consulting, LLC.

I have had a fortunate journey in the DE&I space, but to this day the sports industry remains my first love. It is where I gained my most substantive experience as well as where I built, and have enjoyed, my best professional relationships, many of which have become lifelong friendships. I am proud to include Jason in that pool. I had the honor of meeting Jason in 2014 while I was the chief diversity officer (CDO) at Major League Baseball where I was responsible for developing and leading the D&I strategy for the entire league and its thirty club markets. It was my first CDO role, and I was completely stressed out about destroying the DE&I foundation built by my predecessor. It takes a village, as an adage goes that is worth its weight in gold, in the sports industry.

Enter Jason, CDO of the USOC, and his brainchild, the Diversity and Inclusion Sports Consortium (DISC). Jason was one of the visionaries and co-founders of DISC, a coalition of DE&I leaders from every major sports organization in North America. This is no small feat, as you can imagine, And yet Jason was able to convince all of us of its need, utility, and the potential impact we could have on the industry. Jason was uniquely able to establish individual connections with all of us through his passion for the subject matter and his general unselfishness as he readily shared his unique approach to DE&I. Jason was deep-diving into data and metrics in DE&I well before they could be Googled. He created programs with detailed scorecards designed not only to hold himself accountable to his role but also to hold his organization accountable to the agenda. Jason's approach (one many of us DISC members riffed upon and leveraged) and DISC influenced many of our approaches to DE&I in sports, moving beyond the performative to the quantifiable impact. New developmental programs were established for existing and aspiring diverse professionals in sports, DE&I education became the norm, and social justice conversations became a bit less daunting (albeit they still remain challenging, but at least we have started).

There is no silver bullet, outlining a perfect way to strategize and deploy DE&I. First of all, every organization is different, and the culture and leadership are incredible influencers on DE&I's success at the company. Second, I know firsthand how difficult it is to find practical advice and guidance when starting a DE&I program. Much of the information out there is either overly aspirational without any real practical or tactical insight *or* overladen with a heavy dose of metrics/ data that only skim the surface by overemphasizing hiring and representation without consideration of promotion, development, marketing, CSR investments, and so forth. Finally, even the good information out there is remarkably dense and (inadvertently) presupposes that DE&I departments are naturally the size of a small army à la Amazon, Google, or Starbucks. Spoiler alert: most are not.

These challenges lend themselves to the beauty of this book. It provides a comprehensive roadmap for either the DE&I professional just starting out, the seasoned expert seeking a new prospective, or anyone in between. Jason has successfully broken down all the components of a successful DE&I program that lays the responsibility not only of the DE&I leader (as most how-tos do) but also of the organization itself. From his emphasis and insights on engaging internal stakeholders, as well as positioning of DE&I as organizational change to your own self-care as a professional in a very tough discipline, *Diversity and Inclusion Matters* weaves a comprehensive narrative that will allow any professional with the appropriate dedication, will, and finesse to drive diversity, equity, and inclusion throughout their organization. And the individual chapters equally stand on their own for the professional looking for guidance on a particular subject to help push them to the next level of their DE&I strategy.

Where the book shines is Jason's clear explanations of the role of data in DE&I. We live in a world where data is king. The use of this data has not always been clear or robust enough to allow for systemic overhaul. For most organizations, DE&I data usually stops at representation and Employee Resource Groups(ERG) participation numbers with targets set to hit achievable and less-scary goals, Jason shares a detailed look at the opportunities available to leverage data beyond representation and optics, moves toward analyzing the numbers to set logical but challenging goals, and most uniquely, explains how to measure the elusive and subjective idea of inclusion.

So why this book versus others? Why not just conduct an internet search for plans or reach out to a colleague on LinkedIn? Because Jason's work is proven. His methodology has made, and continues to make, an impact. His work remains intact at every organization he has been a part of. This is not to say that his work has saved the world (all seasoned DE&I professionals know that is not the goal).

This discipline is meant to set into motion cultural and systemic change that will allow diverse voices to find professional equity in the workplace in a manner that is sustainable and a proverbial win, not only for the individuals impacted, but for the organization as a whole. Jason's work has accomplished just that. He has pushed organizations to think about DE&I holistically and set foundations that have allowed them to embed the DE&I agenda in their business to build upon it as a strategic imperative versus a social initiative (the latter, while important, is merely one piece of the puzzle, but I'll wait for Jason to tackle that in his next book). This book gives you the tools to start that journey.

The DE&I field is crowded now. The last year has seen companies invest in DE&I in ways never imagined by those of us who have been in the trenches a bit longer. But the reality is that change is remarkably slow. While it is great to see more diversity in marketing campaigns and to hear about companies creating more developmental and celebratory programs, sustainability remains elusive. The real work involves the day-to-day management, accountability, and investment in driving that cultural shift that normalizes and empowers diverse perspectives and people at all levels of the organization. *Diversity and Inclusion Matters* outlines how to get the real work done and accomplished in a way that allows it to live well beyond changing CDOs or business priorities. Investing in this goal goes well beyond investing in your company's agenda. It's an investment in your own success and, if applied thoughtfully, the success of future professionals and the culture. As my trusted colleague, friend, and someone I continue to call for guidance and perspective, Jason has created this book with a voice reflecting empathy, intellectual curiosity, and expertise I trust implicitly. I hope you enjoy it and get as much out of it as I have. I wish you the best of luck on your journeys. You have the right companion piece by your side.

Pa'lante,
Renee E. Tirado, Esq.

Part I

The CAPE Process

Not everything that is faced can be changed, but nothing can be changed until it is faced.

—James A. Baldwin

Chapter 1

How to Become
an Exceptional DE&I
Organization

Four Shades of Brown

When my daughter Piper was in her second year of college, she came to me and said, "Dad, look at this!" Piper put a makeup advertisement under my nose and said, "This makeup company makes twenty shades of makeup for White people and only four shades of brown! This company needs a diversity and inclusion program!" We both laughed, but the reality of this statement hit too close to home. For my daughter, her brown skin is both beautiful and a reminder of the work we need to do.

This experience with my daughter was an example of diversity, equity, and inclusion (DE&I), both literally and metaphorically. DE&I work is about more than four shades of brown. The makeup ad provides an entry point to the framework I use to think about diversity, equity, and inclusion.

Using the ad, I considered the company that developed the makeup and asked myself some questions related to DE&I.

- **Diversity:** Were any of the company's employees from non-dominant ethnic groups, genders, or countries? Did anyone working on this ad or product line have brown skin?
- **Equity:** Did any of the employees of the company realize the disparity in the ad?
- **Inclusion:** If so, did they believe they could speak up?

I also wondered about the process this company used to make decisions. Was there a group of employees who sat together in a room to approve the ad? Was it possible that a group of employees saw the ad, and everyone agreed that there were only four shades of brown skin? Did they decide that four shades were all that was needed for people with brown skin, but twenty variations were needed for White people? Did they give any thought to the many different cultures in the world and how they use makeup?

DE&I work is about pointing out these types of disparities *and* developing solutions.

The challenge is not simply to develop an equal number of shades for people with brown skin. Rather, it is to change a company's culture so employees can recognize the disparity and see the opportunity. The more I thought about this experience with my daughter, the more I began to think about the opportunity that DE&I brings to companies. When companies have a great product and start to think there are *more than four shades of brown*, they expand their perspective and, therefore, their potential for success.

I wanted to do this work because it was a way to let people know there are more than four shades of brown, so to speak. The world is a diverse place full of people with different skin tones, identities, backgrounds, and experiences. Inclusion is about developing a culture that prevents moments like the one my daughter pointed out and about realizing that developing more than four shades of brown is an opportunity to expand a company's customer base.

The Importance of DE&I Now

Diversity, equity, and inclusion have become an imperative for nearly every major corporation, educational institution, and government agency in the United States, as well as globally. The many calls for substantial systemic change and protests supporting social justice in the United States require that all organizations and institutions must do more than make pledges – they must install the practices that make real change. To introduce you to your first Jason-ism: *Audio must match video.*

JASON-ISM
Audio must match video.

Matching audio with video is part of the landscape for change to achieve your DE&I goals. It means that the verbal commitments a company makes must be in sync with the company's actions. Words alone aren't enough; they need to be followed up with a financial commitment. An article on the McKinsey & Company website titled "It's a start: Fortune 1000 companies commit $66 billion to racial-equity initiatives"[1] shows that there are now major financial commitments to align with the statements to advance racial equity. This is a great start and points to much-needed change.

As a result of the growing importance of DE&I, the number of job postings for DE&I positions continue to rise globally. As Figure 1.1 shows, the United Kingdom saw an incredible increase of 106% from 2018 to 2019.[2]

Even more recently, CNBC reported an even greater demand for these positions in the United States, stating, "Demand is rising for chief diversity officers across the U.S., with job postings for diversity and inclusion roles on Glassdoor up 55% since early June 2020 when the conversation around racial tensions – and corporate America's response – took center stage."[3] In early 2021, Bloomberg reported that job postings for chief diversity officers were up 75%.[4]

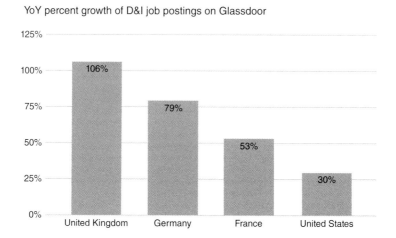

Figure 1.1 YoY Percent Growth of DE&I Job Postings on Glassdoor.
Source: Redrawn from data from Gilchrist, 2020.

This demand has created an even greater need and urgency for tools, such as the CAPE process. It is a tool you will be able to use for your continued success and benefit from the return on investment that results from it. The upward trend in chief diversity officer position openings is indicative of the importance corporations are putting on the need to be socially responsible and have a diverse workforce.

A Diverse Workforce Will Have Tension

What does it mean to have a diverse workforce? It simply means that your workplace looks like the world we live in, meaning it will share the same tension around politics, race, gender, religion, sexual orientation, and so on. A company with a good DE&I program is one in which people feel empowered to speak up, in spite of the tension. Even successful DE&I programs have tension because people don't always agree on issues or policies. Sometimes that will make you feel as though you aren't doing a good enough job. Let me provide you with an example of how tension is a necessary part of DE&I.

JASON-ISM

Good DE&I programs are not without tension. DE&I programs will have tension because inclusive and equitable work cultures create an environment where people can speak up and disagree without retribution. I am more concerned when no one speaks up on contentious issues.

In 2016, a colleague that was the chief diversity officer at a very large tech company called me and said, "I have a problem, and I need your help. We sent out an email after the presidential election as we knew emotions were running high and people were very concerned about Donald Trump being the president." My colleague told me that as soon as the email went out, they began receiving emails from African American employees. The employees were questioning why the company had not also sent out an email in support of Black Lives Matter. In exasperation, this particular chief diversity officer said, "I am getting it from all sides. I can't win."

I could fully appreciate that my colleague felt as though their work were being criticized. Being a chief diversity officer can be very isolating. Many times other executive leaders don't understand this concept and the non-executive employees often have expectations that can't always be met. I did not want to diminish how they were feeling, but I told them, "Your program is working." The fact that employees were contacting the chief diversity officer meant that they felt empowered to speak up. Inclusion means employees can share their concerns without retribution. It means we can talk openly about sensitive subjects like race, ethnicity, sexual orientation, gender, ability, and many other identities and subjects. Tension is a natural part of those conversations, which is why good DE&I programs have tension.

It is not unusual to see something similar after sexual harassment training. People mistakenly think that sexual harassment training will reduce complaints because employees will stop the harassing behavior. While training can reduce occurrences of harassment, we typically see an *increase* in complaints after sexual harassment training. Why? Because when sexual harassment training is done correctly, it reduces the behavior of harassment, but more importantly, it signals to employees that they do *not* have to accept inappropriate behavior and that there is a process to protect and support them.

Effective DE&I programs have ongoing training and policies to limit bias and bad behavior, and they also have clear processes for addressing complaints. In the early stages of a DE&I program, ongoing training is proof of the organization's commitment. Cultures take time to change, so ongoing training is necessary to help employees understand the change and expectations. Once they do, employees working in inclusive cultures will let you know how they think you're doing.

DE&I Officers Need a Broad Range of Skills

Over the years, when I tell people I work in DE&I, I am often asked, "What do you do on a daily basis?" Even people who understand the goal of DE&I don't really know what it looks like in action. My response is that it is like being the producer for an orchestra. In an orchestra, the conductor leads the musicians, but the producer has to find the individuals to play a diverse range of instruments to get the music right. As a DE&I officer, you need to be able to influence each individual employee and understand the organization's *music*, but you don't get to make the final decisions. That is left to the CEO, who is like the conductor of the company. In that way, DE&I is like any other behind-the-scenes job – and no one notices you until something goes wrong. Problems are inevitable, and in order to be prepared for them, the major skills a DE&I officer will need are influence, relationship building, data analysis, and patience, because the DE&I officer will be called out and put on the hot seat.

Here are some common issues that DE&I professionals have to address:

- **The leadership team is not diverse.** I hear this all the time. I cannot count the times I have heard, "If the company was committed to diversity, the leadership team would be more diverse." This is true, but drastic change in the diversity of the leadership team will not happen in a short period of time. It doesn't happen quickly because that would require high turnover in leadership positions and high turnover at any level of a company is a bad thing – especially the leadership team. In Chapter 5, I will give you some ways to address this, but for now, I'll leave you with another one of my Jasonisms: One of the biggest challenges for DE&I professionals is unrealistic expectations. The skills you need are data analysis, patience, and the ability to articulate realistic expectations.

- **There is no diversity on the board.** Here again, a significant change in the demographic makeup of the board takes time. A drastic change in any corporate board in a short period of time is typically a bad thing. If you don't believe me, ask the people at General Electric.[5] Their board shake-up was a response to doing poorly, not the result of a high-performing organization. The chief diversity officer (CDO) cannot make decisions about the makeup of the board but is held accountable for its lack of diversity. There have been changes and legal requirements to create more board diversity, but these changes take time and, sometimes, mandates from the government.[6] Again, the skills you need are data analysis, patience, and the ability to help set realistic expectations.

- **If the company were committed to equity, women would be paid fairly.** This is true, but the majority of hiring and salary decisions that created this problem of inequity were made before you started. Additionally, when you bring this to the attention of the organization, the changes to salary won't happen the same day. There are many constraints, real and sometimes political, and the CDO doesn't control all the variables. The skills you will need are relationship building, data analysis, and thick skin. The truth is that no one should have to wait another day to be paid fairly, but it is also not your fault. You do not have the authority to change salaries, but, trust me, you will be held accountable.

- **The marketing ads look racist.** This one happens all the time. Ask the people at H&M, Target, Dolce & Gabbana, or Estee Lauder just to name a few.[7] Here, again, not every ad is given to the CDO for review and approval, but if an ad lands poorly, they will call on you to fix it. The skills you need here are relationship building, writing good apologies, and staying current on events.

- **African American, Women, Latinx, or fill in the blank employees are not being promoted.** There is a long list of companies that struggle in this space "For instance, at Google, only 2.6% of leadership and 2.4% of technical workers are Black. At Facebook, Black people make up only 3.1% of those in leadership roles and 1.5% of those in

The Wide Range of Job Responsiblilities of DE&I Officers

• Counselor and advisor • Business strategist • Staffing support at all levels • Workforce development and succession planning • Creation of diverse talent both at headquarters and in the business units • Training and education • Compliance • Policies, especially as they apply to women and a diverse and inclusive workforce, work/life, and leadership • Recruiting • Innovation	• Diversity council and affinity group relations • Marketing and marketplace development • Communications • Sponsorships • Partnerships • Community and philanthoropy • Supplier diversity and inclusion • Global business • Ethics • Government contracting • Other issues (e.g., labor relations and culture)

Figure 1.2 Job Responsibilities of DE&I Officers.

technical roles."[8] The lack of promotions is likely an indicator of a deeper problem, and one that has been going on before you started. It may not take that long to diagnose but putting in a solution never moves fast enough, and you will be put on the spot to fix it. The skills you will need are data analytics and relationship building.

There is a long and varied list of skills and abilities that a DE&I officer needs. Figure 1.2 is a snapshot of things I had to understand and address over my career, and I can assure you that the list here is far from complete.

A day in the life of a DE&I professional is multi-dimensional. Many days I have started my morning with an unconscious bias training, taken meetings to support employees who may be experiencing discrimination, reviewed and edited press releases/social media postings, created an invitation for partnership with an external partner, supported a sales meeting, reviewed/edited a company policy, and ended the day by writing a blog post. In a single day, I've been a trainer, counselor, communications director, strategic partnership manager, salesperson, legal analyst, and writer.

Why DE&I Programs Fail

Despite the increase in diversity officers and good intentions, many companies are struggling to achieve their DE&I goals and to develop successful programs because they have been asked to do too much in too little time.

I recently received a call from a person who had transitioned from the head of sales to CDO of a global company with more than 40,000 employees. The person had done very well as a sales director, but that experience did not prepare them to be the CDO. This person found me on LinkedIn and contacted me, needing my help. The opportunity to be CDO was a significant promotion, so I don't blame them for wanting the opportunity. Additionally, prior to the promotion, this person had worked to help move the company toward establishing a DE&I program. What they were finding out is that making the argument to company leaders to start a DE&I program and leading a DE&I program on a daily basis were two different things. I get a lot of calls like this from diversity officers who are struggling and don't know what to do on a regular basis. These calls come from high-profile companies, sports organizations, and technology companies.

Without any background or experience, these individuals, who are otherwise very successful, simply did not know where to start. Some of these calls were from individuals who were overwhelmed, and they had not even been on the job a month. They had established the need for diversity, equity, and inclusion but did not know where to go from there. They needed a bridge. I introduced them to the CAPE process:

- Collect the demographic data.
- Analyze it.
- Plan development.
- Execute it.

I explain to them that if you start with an overly broad generalization like "We need to recruit diverse candidates," you will quickly become overwhelmed. Generally, most DE&I departments are not staffed nor designed to oversee every single hire. Overly broad goals will undermine your success.

Everyone has some understanding of DE&I, but that doesn't mean everyone knows how to do the job. Roughly half of S&P 500 companies employ a CDO, and 63% of those had been appointed or promoted to their roles within the past three years, according to a 2019 study by Russell Reynolds Associates.[9]

The short length of service is symptomatic of good intent but challenging situations. This is exacerbated by the fact that many of these diversity officers lack previous experience. They may have done very well in their previous non-diversity positions, but that doesn't always translate to successful execution of an impactful DE&I program.

A *Fortune* magazine article titled "Chief Diversity Officers Are Set Up To Fail"[10] outlined some key reasons why CDOs are struggling to succeed. The article indicated that the majority of the CDOs were new to the role and often were given other responsibilities in addition to their diversity work. Also, they tended to have limited power over decisions that affected diversity in the company. A large majority of these CDOs did not even have access to the kind of data they needed to make a difference. Additionally, the CDOs reported that diversity, equity, and inclusion work ranked last in terms of perceived importance by company leaders. You can see how this would make it impossible to make any measurable gains in DE&I work (Figure 1.3).

The How: CAPE Foundation for Successful DE&I Programs

With all these challenges, there is a way forward. CAPE is an easy to use foundational tool based on a straightforward process (Figure 1.4). Let's look a little further into each step in the CAPE process:

1. Collecting data is critical to having a successful program. Knowing what data to collect, and when, is critical to knowing if you are going in the right direction. At the end of the day, every chief diversity officer has to show numbers.
2. Analyzing the data is equally important. Once you collect the right data, you will need to analyze it in a meaningful way across the organization in order to make an actionable plan with obtainable and reasonable goals.
3. Plan. Having a plan based on the measurable DE&I data that outlines the challenges and opportunities of your organization will help you effectively manage your time and resources.
4. Execute. After you build a plan on data, it is time to execute on your plan.

Why DE&I Leaders Fail	Key Findings	The Reasons
They are the newcomers in the organization	Majority of the CDOs have recently been promoted to that position	• Only one-third of CDOs working in S&P 500 index companies have experience. The vast majority are new to the job.
They do not get the respect they need for promotion and adoption of their initiatives	No positional authority	• They are frequently asked to pick up additional responsibilities outside of their diversity work. • Over half of them do not have the resources they need to be successful in their role.
They don't have the data they need to make a difference	65% did not have the data to support their work	• In a data-driven role, they are woefully ill prepared to make decisions, since only a little over a third of the CDOs had the employee demographic survey information they needed to support their work.
Other leaders aren't on board	100% put DE&I last on priorities	• All of the leaders reported that diversity and inclusion came in last on a list of the business priorities for their companies.

Figure 1.3 Reasons DE&I Leaders Fail.

13

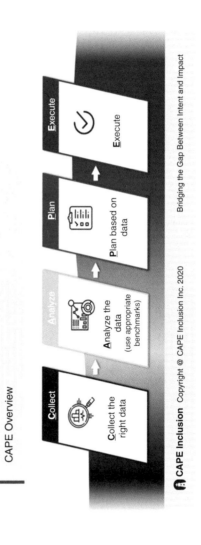

Figure 1.4 The CAPE Process Overview.

Source: Reproduced with permission of CAPE Inclusion Inc.

5. Because you started with collecting data, you will be able to assess your progress, adjust if necessary, and measure your success – ROI.

The CAPE process gives you and your company a previously unseen way forward. Chapters 2 through 6 will further explain each step in the CAPE process.

KEY POINTS

- Good DE&I programs have tension because inclusive and equitable work cultures create an environment where people can speak up and disagree without retribution.
- DE&I officers need a range of skills to help them set realistic expectations within the organization.
- Overly broad goals will undermine your success.
- The CAPE process can help you move forward by bringing focus to your efforts.

Notes

1. One of the insights derived from the McKinsey Global survey on technology strategy, in data analyzed by the McKinsey Institute for Black Economic Development, is the commitment to impact Black-equity by Fortune 500 companies on the heels of the killing of George Floyd. Titled "It's a start: Fortune 500 companies commit $66 billion to racial-equity initiatives," the full document was published on December 4, 2020 and was accessed on April 5, 2021 at https://www.mckinsey.com/featured-insights/coronavirus-leading-through-the-crisis/charting-the-path-to-the-next-normal/its-a-start-fortune-1000-companies-commit-66-billion-to-racial-equity-initiatives

2. To start off the new year on January 1, 2020, Karen Gilchrist, a CNBC correspondent, published an article on the anticipated rise in demand for diversity and inclusion professionals, entitled "Hiring experts expect demand for this role to surge in 2020 – and it can pay a median of $126,000." Accessed on April 5, 2020 at https://www.cnbc.com/2020/01/02/demand-for-diversity-and-inclusion-professionals-set-to-rise-in-2020.html

3. CNBC continued its coverage of the DE&I professional space with an article by Seema Mody on July 29, 2020, entitled "Diversity officers are in demand across corporate America but are often underpaid," and raising cautions about challenges to the role. Accessed on April 5, 2020 at https://www.cnbc.com/2020/07/29/diversity-officers-are-in-demand-at-us-companies-but-often-underpaid.html.

4. A recent article by Denise Hamilton (January 18, 2021) in Bloomberg Opinion suggests that burnout may be one of the pitfalls of working as a professional in the diversity and inclusion space. She cautions that the work can lead to burnout rather than promotion due to a number of factors, including recruiting diversity officers from Human Resources who have a lack of experience in the DE&I profession. Accessed on April 4, 2021 at https://www.bloomberg.com/opinion/articles/2021-01-18/don-t-let-chief-diversity-officer-be-a-dead-end-job

5. In a February 2018 article in the *Washington Post*, Jena McGregor reports on why GE was engaged in a major overhaul of its board of directors following a lengthy list of struggles. Accessed on April 7, 2021 at https://www.washingtonpost.com/news/on-leadership/wp/2018/02/27/why-ge-is-making-a-dramatic-overhaul-to-its-board-of-directors/

6. The Harvard Law School Forum on Corporate Governance published a memorandum by Michael Hatcher and Weldon Lathan on May 12, 2020, about how a dozen or more states were enacting requirements for corporations and businesses to enhance diversity on their boards of directors. The article details the actions in California, Illinois, New York, and Pennsylvania among others. Accessed on April 7, 2021 at https://corpgov.law.harvard.edu/2020/05/12/states-are-leading-the-charge-to-corporate-boards-diversify/

7. The seven most embarrassing branding mistakes of 2018 were chronicled by Brit Morse in an article for INC. The majority were culturally, racially, or ethnically insensitive and offensive. Accessed on April 7, 2020, at https://www.inc.com/brit-morse/2018-biggest-marketing-branding-fails.html

8. Sam Dean and Johana Bhuiyan, writing for the *Los Angeles Times* on June 14, 2020, called out the tech industry for lacking diversity and for being far less than transparent about it, entitled "Why are Black and Latino people still left out of the tech industry?" the article primarily reports on diversity at Google, who released the data on racial and gender diversity of their workforce demographic data in 2014, but the lack of diversity throughout the tech industry is evidenced. Accessed on April 7, 2020 at https://www.latimes.com/business/technology/story/2020-06-24/tech-started-publicly-taking-lack-of-diversity-seriously-in-2014-why-has-so-little-changed-for-black-workers

9. Tina Shah Paikeday, "A Leader's Guide: Finding and Keeping Your Next Chief Diversity Officer," Russell Reynolds. Accessed June 23, 2021, at: https://www.russellreynolds.com/insights/thought-leadership/a-leaders-guide-finding-and-keeping-your-next-chief-diversity-officer

10. Chip Cutter and Lauren Weber commented on the future of work for, and the turnover of, Diversity Officers on July 13, 2020 in an article for the *Wall Street Journal*. They noted, "It's one of the hottest jobs in America – and it has a revolving door." Accessed on April 7, 2021 at https://www.wsj.com/articles/demand-for-chief-diversity-officers-is-high-so-is-turnover-11594638000

Chapter 2

DE&I Fundamentals, CAPE, and Organizational Change

Overwhelmed and Needing a Process

When I was a graduate student at the University of Wyoming, I remember being overwhelmed with the thought of starting my thesis. It had to be over 100 pages and, in some way, add to the field of study. At that point in my life, I had never even written more than ten pages, so writing 100 pages seemed like an impossible task for me. I remember thinking, *Why did I even start this graduate program?!?* There was no way I could write 100 pages of anything. I had no idea where to start or even what to start researching. With my history of being a slow reader and terrible writer, the task was way too big, and I stopped doing anything.

As luck would have it, a faculty member, Dr. Garth Massey, saw me struggling and told me a story I will never forget. I often reflect on this story when I begin to feel immobilized by a task that seems too big.

Dr. Massey shared a parable with me about a parent, their young child, and a large walnut tree.

As this story goes, the child (who was about six years old) was called out to the front yard of the home where there was a large walnut tree. The parent pointed to the walnuts that had fallen out of the tree and said to the small child, "You need to pick up all these walnuts."

Apparently, this tree was quite large, and there were walnuts every-where. I did a quick Google search and found that a mature walnut tree can produce up to 350 lbs. of nuts. The average nut weighs bet-ween five to ten grams and there are 454 grams in a pound. You can do the math here, but that is a lot of walnuts!

As you can imagine, the young child looked at the tree, looked at the walnuts all over the front yard, and was immediately overwhelmed by the task. The small child knew immediately this task was too big and they would never be able to pick up all the walnuts. Without responding, the child began to cry. The child was overwhelmed by the task. I could relate to this child as I, too, was immobilized by the task of writing my graduate theses. It was just too big.

The parent said to the child, "Go into the shed and get some string and seven stakes."

The parent placed seven stakes evenly around the tree. They then tied the string from the tree to each of the seven stakes creating what looked like seven pieces of pie. They then looked at the child and said, "All you have to do is clear one section of the pie every day for seven days. At the end of seven days, you will have picked up all the walnuts."

This helped me to get started on my graduate thesis, as it reminded me that you don't write the thesis in one day. Most importantly you have to break the task into manageable pieces in order to get started. You need a plan.

Over my career, I have launched four diversity, equity, and inclusion (DE&I) programs in four different industries, and I have often reminded myself of this story to help me get started and keep the faith that my work will bear fruit. When you start a DE&I program, there is typically little budget, no staff, and everyone wants everything fixed on day one. Things move slowly, and at times it feels as though nothing is moving. To keep momentum and track my progress, at the start of any DE&I program I remind myself and the people I'm working with to not get overwhelmed, stick to the plan, stay flexible, and realize we have been given a huge task. Much like the parent's advice in this parable, the CAPE process was designed to help you stay on task and identify which section needs to be picked up first. Not everything will get done on day one, but keep working on the piece you need to fix on that day. Walnuts will keep falling, but you can use the CAPE process, create a plan, and stick to it.

In this chapter, I'll cover the basics of a DE&I program and talk about the two central aspects of DE&I work:

1. Establishing a shared language for DE&I
2. Recruitment and retention

Throughout this chapter, you will be introduced to a model for managing the change that DE&I brings into any organization so that you can set some stakes into the ground of your DE&I work.

The Basics of Every DE&I Program

Starting a DE&I program can feel overwhelming, a bit like that child standing at the foot of the walnut tree. Where to begin with such a huge task in front of you? Remember, this is also a big organizational shift for the company; therefore, much like the story above, start with simple tools and basics.

The goal of any DE&I program is cultural change. To change the culture of the organization, you need a shared language and understanding of where the company is going. I recommend two simple tools. First, take a moment to make sure everyone is using the same definitions (language) for diversity, equity, and inclusion. The second is using some basic organizational change theory. I use a model of organizational change developed by Jeff Hiatt called ADKAR. I will provide a simple understanding of the change management model that will prove to be very effective.

Shared Language (Basic Definitions)

By committing to a collective understanding of these definitions you can set expectations and know everyone is using the same fundamental understanding. Below are examples, but I would develop definitions that resonate with your company or organization.

- **Diversity:** *What do we look like?* Diversity is about reflecting the mixture of differences and similarities that we find in the world and acknowledging the related tension as we strive to develop more inclusive and high-performing environments.
- **Equity:** *How do we treat each other and what are our policies to ensure equity?* Equity is the principle of creating full access and removing barriers to participation. Equity is fair treatment, access, opportunity, and advancement for all people, while at the same time striving to identify and eliminate barriers that prevent the full participation of some groups.
- **Inclusion:** *Why we stay?* Inclusion is about making people feel welcomed and valued. Inclusion is retention.

DE&I Change Management Model versus Diversity Training

Diversity training is part of how you create a more diverse and inclusive work environment, but it is not a solution in and of itself. A one-time training, whether it's 45 minutes or a whole day, will not change the culture of the organization or one's views. Diversity training is part of the process the company will use to create the needed change for the organization. In 2019 a *Harvard Business Review* article stated that virtually all Fortune 500 companies offer diversity training to their employees.[1] Despite this "since 2000, 99% of Fortune 500 companies have paid settlements in at least one discrimination or sexual harassment lawsuit, according to a report from Good Jobs First, and that's not including the cases without a public record or incidents victims didn't report."[2]

So why doesn't diversity training work? The biggest challenge for diversity programs is unrealistic expectations! Think about it: It would be impossible to teach someone calculus in a one-hour session. Yet, we think a one-hour mandatory session on diversity will teach employees everything they need to know about race, ethnicity, discrimination, privilege, the LGBTQ+ community, persons with disabilities, unconscious bias, and so on. Even if you did a two-week, all-day mandatory session, you could not reasonably think all the items listed above could be taught, and no one would ever assume everyone would retain all that information.

> **JASON-ISM**
> One of the biggest challenges for diversity programs is unrealistic expectations.

The best way to get organizational change and create an inclusive environment is to use organizational change models and principles. The one I recommend is the ADKAR model created by Prosci founder, Jeff Hiatt.[3] ADKAR is an acronym that stands for awareness, desire, knowledge, ability, and reinforcement. I've adapted Hiatt's model to address the specific needs of DE&I (Figure 2.1).

The adaptation from a diversity-training model to a model that supports change at the organizational level is necessary because DE&I is broad, complicated, and requires lots of repetition. For example, I could have a very good understanding of race, but that would not mean I also have an equally good understanding of anything to do with people with disabilities. Moreover, even within the concept of race, an understanding of the experience of African Americans would not mean I have an understanding of the experience of Indigenous people. Each of the concepts would require its own model to increase understanding.

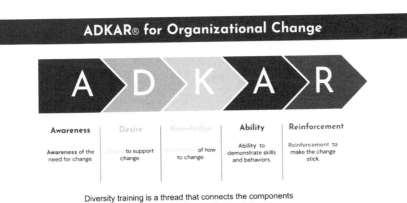

ADKAR® for Organizational Change

Awareness	Desire	Knowledge	Ability	Reinforcement
Awareness of the need for change.	Desire to support change.	Knowledge of how to change.	Ability to demonstrate skills and behaviors.	Reinforcement to make the change stick.

Diversity training is a thread that connects the components of the ADKAR® model for organizational change.

Figure 2.1 ADKAR® model for organizational change.

Source: ADKAR is a registered trademark of Prosci, Inc. Used with Permission.

Recruitment and Retention

I remember a call I received from a CDO who had been on the job about 10 months, and nothing was going their way. They were the head of DE&I for a large tech company. They were not sure what to do, the initiatives they tried were not working, and they were convinced the employee resource group (ERG) leaders hated them. The ERG leaders were questioning all the decisions they did make, and there was no way to show progress. This person realized that as CDO, they were supposed to influence every hire made by the organization and help the CEO and every other senior leader set expectations and goals on DE&I. They were coming to the end of their first year, and they were going to be held responsible if the goals were not met. On top of that, they needed to set more goals for year two of the fledgling program. This was overwhelming, to say the least, and generally not all of this was going to get done. They wanted my help, and because I had seen this before, I knew I could offer some good guidance.

Generally, I found there were certain issues that continued to come up. First, there was no manual to help them run a DE&I program. Second, they were overwhelmed by all the things that needed to be fixed. Third, the company had unrealistic expectations of what a DE&I program could do and of the timeline necessary to make the desired change.

The combination of these three issues make it impossible to be successful. When there is an overwhelming list of things to be done, the expectations are unrealistic, and if there is no manual to help you show results, you will struggle. It is a no-win situation for both the diversity officer and the company. As I always say, the toughest part of a DE&I job is unrealistic expectations.

The solution for this CDO, and what I have helped others understand, is that most of these issues arise from making DE&I goals too theoretical and impractical. I told them that there are two main things that all DE&I programs do: recruitment and retention of employees (Figure 2.2). Approximately 90% of the work falls in these two categories. As a company, you are either recruiting staff or you are trying to retain staff. Your DE&I program may also include students or customers, but the fundamental goal is the same. You are recruiting students and customers, or you are retaining them. Understanding this principle will make your DE&I program highly impactful. Additionally, because

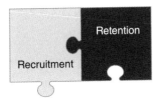

Figure 2.2 The Recruitment Retention Link for DE&I.

you've narrowed the parameters, it's easy to figure out the numbers, the quantitative data, that you need to track and report your success.

JASON-ISM
There are two main things that all DE&I programs do: recruitment and retention.

Using the framework of recruitment and retention will help prioritize the many objectives and goals DE&I officers are given. By understanding how to frame your DE&I work and using CAPE, the puzzle pieces will start to make sense, and you can stay focused, thus building an exceptional organization.

The practical reason for categorizing DE&I work into recruitment and retention is to create a simple matrix to prioritize your resources and the work you need to do. For example, when I developed the Diversity Scorecards for the United States Olympic and Paralympic Committee (USOPC), I used this basic framing. You can see the Diversity Scorecards on the Team USA website, but I have created the CAPE Diversity scorecard that is more widely applicable regardless of industry (Figure 2.3). The USOPC is made up of over 50 independent national governing bodies (NGBs) representing each sport within the Olympic and Paralympic movement. The CEO of USOPC at that time wanted a simple way to measure the DE&I work. This was no small task because each NGB is an independent nonprofit with their own board and leadership team, and I was required to help each of them create a plan and execute it. When I started, I had no staff and little budget. At that time the only DE&I-focused program USOPC had was called FLAME. I was told to take over the FLAME program, but the HR director at that time refused to transition the budget to run

	Diversity				
	Total Employees	Percentage of Women Employed	Percentage of Women Available Benchmark	Percentage to Benchmark	Hires to Reach Benchmark in 2020
Executive / Senior Level Officials and Managers	27	15%	16%	93%	0
First/Mid-Level Officials and Managers	109	12%	16%	77%	4
Professional	137	23%	22%	104%	0
Technicians	7	29%	29%	100%	0
Administrative Support Workers	60	8%	23%	35%	9
Craft Workers	10	20%	24%	83%	0
Service Workers	47	19%	32%	60%	6
Total	397	16%	46%	72%	19

Figure 2.3 A Sample CAPE DE&I Insights scorecard allows for easy-to-visualize DE&I solutions.

Source: United States Olympic & Paralympic Committee.

the program. So, there I was trying to launch a DE&I program with little budget and given a program to run with no budget. I was eventually able to get the FLAME budget transferred to my department, and I did run a successful program, but needless to say there was a lot of work to be done and little support.

The USOPC had made a commitment to DE&I, but they didn't know where or how to start. I built Diversity Scorecards to show the diversity of every NGB within the USOPC and compared them against one another in a way that also valued the uniqueness of each sport.

This simple way of framing DE&I around recruitment and retention meant everyone had usable data, and it helped them understand what needed to be done. By having the demographic data in an easy-to-digest format about the employees and where they were in the company by department and level, the US Olympic and Paralympic Team leaders had a good understanding of the company's needs for recruitment and retention. Therefore, we set up programs and priorities that could be successful. We identified where we needed recruitment (diversity) efforts and where we needed retention (inclusion) efforts.

One of the successes of using the Diversity and Inclusion scorecards while I was at the United States Olympic and Paralympic team was that I was able to quickly show the CEO that the organization had a lack of diversity at the director level and above. In response to this, I created and implemented a program to increase diversity. It was designed so that hiring managers could quickly understand that they needed to interview four candidates, two of whom needed to be women or People of Color, and by doing so the odds of hiring a woman or Person of Color was 50%. It created no advantage for any one candidate. (Chapter 6 has a more detailed explanation about this process, which I call the 4-2-50 program.) This simple approach to recruitment leveled the playing field because it helps hiring managers overcome bias. At USOPC, the outcome was a threefold increase in the hiring of women and People of Color at the director level or above. This was well received because I was able to identify the problem and provide a specific solution, using the CAPE approach of collect, analyze, plan, and execute.

Another example of the power of the Diversity and Inclusion Scorecards was a time when I sat down with the person tasked with DE&I for the US Soccer Federation. This person had been with US Soccer for many years, but they were not a DE&I professional and had been given the responsibility of US Soccer's DE&I program as a project. The person was feeling very overwhelmed and said to me, "There's no way we could be successful because look at USA Basketball, we are never going to get there!" My response was, "Being like USA Basketball should not be your goal. USA Basketball is an example of over-representation. There are a lot of Black/African Americans but no Asians, no Latinx, and too few women on the staff." I showed them the US Soccer Diversity Scorecard and said, "This will help you set goals and identify the best use of your time. You can't fix everything at once. You have limited resources and bandwidth. Pick a recruitment or retention effort and build a plan for your organization." When I made this suggestion, I could see the relief on their face because now they could see how to develop a specific plan with measurable outcomes that could be shared with the leadership team.

Surveys and Their Limitations

Surveys are commonly used to support employee retention efforts. They are easy to administer and quickly yield data regarding employees' feelings on a myriad of subjects. Many companies frequently use this tool, but I would argue that the results are often an illusion, inaccurate, and not a good indication of how the company should move on important matters for underrepresented employees.

The biggest reason surveys are not helpful is that they are based on majority rule and that by definition is biased against underrepresented groups.

What company will change their approach or their culture based on a small percentage of responses? Nobody does that. But if you think about it, you can have several departments that have one Person of Color or one woman, and if nine people love whatever policy you are polling, and one person hates it, you won't change it because it looks like 90% of people like it.

If you have four People of Color and all of them say they hate the policy or are unhappy with the manager based on that person's behavior toward them, but the other six people are happy, you still have 60% of satisfied workers. There is also the question of trust. If you are the only African American in a department and you are treated poorly, you know it would be a risk to put that in an anonymous survey. If you don't trust your manager or leadership team, you won't be honest on a survey because any negative response will be attributed to you. No one will give honest answers if they feel their direct manager will know who gave them critical scores.

If the interpretation of the survey is always based on majority rule, when you have a few People of Color, or other marginalized groups, their voice through the survey is fundamentally minimized. To overcome bias, what most companies do is try to protect the anonymity of the respondents by taking extraordinary measures. So, let's look at the same example: We have ten employees. One person says they don't like the policy you are polling, that gives you one out of ten. That's 10%. But you can't use that data or share it with the leadership team because they would immediately know the respondent in question was a Person of Color, LGBTQ+, and so on. So, what do you do? One strategy many companies use is to combine their responses with another department, a larger department. So, let's combine, for example, marketing with accounting. Therefore, it helps keep the results anonymous. Seems like that would work, right? Wrong. The problem is, if you put them in with accounting, which has twenty employees including three People of Color who are all happy with the policy, you have the same problem. You've just taken somebody who was 10% of a group, put them in a larger group, and now their vote is only 3%. It's actually decreased in importance. You have less reason to do any actionable things, because, guess what, nobody makes changes in policy or procedures or work culture, if you have 97% approval. There's no reason to change, and the only way this process of combining departments works is if all the members of the underrepresented group have the same opinion or response in the survey.

Not only that, you've now confused the data because you put the one Person of Color in another department. So how do you know which manager to deal with? You don't, because you keep combining department results into bigger and bigger datasets. This makes it hard to train the right person because you've promised everybody that the survey is anonymous. Therefore, efforts to keep surveys anonymous make the responses from underrepresented employees less statistically significant. The minute you show up and say, People of Color are not happy, and there's only one Person of Color, everybody knows who it is. The only way you can address their concerns using surveys is to violate any promise of anonymity.

All three of these issues make survey data difficult to act on. Generally, if you say, "The survey shows that there's a problem in the accounting department," the accounting manager's response will typically be: *What is the issue? Who has a problem? Can I see the surveys?* By and large, you can't answer those questions or share the surveys, so it makes it very difficult for you to effectively execute on initiatives related to survey responses. Additionally, the leader of the accounting department could rightly point out that 90% their department is happy. Once you share specifics about the 10% who are unhappy, any leader will quickly figure out who those people are, meaning the survey is no longer anonymous.

For these reasons, it is important to understand how surveys can actually work and why many times they can undermine your efforts. Employees often feel particularly frustrated by surveys. They think, *I tell you every year what's wrong, and you do nothing about it.* The reason you cannot do anything about it is because surveys are anonymous, which makes it difficult for you to present a real picture of the problem. This is why I don't recommend using surveys, because small groups of people will never have their concerns validated or changes made in order to improve employer/employee relations.

More Effective Retention Efforts

Instead of surveys, I would recommend you do some other things. First, look at retention statistics for each department. This is specific data. Do you see high turnover? Unfortunately, much of this data reflects what has already happened, but at least it gives you a data point that you can use. High turnover can be addressed by working with the leader who's creating the problem. There's no need to train everybody and hope the managers who are hurting retention get it.

Quite frankly, most people don't know where to start with a DE&I program, and that can be very detrimental to the overall success of the program. If you are working with qualitative data, you would most likely start your diversity program by sourcing an outside program and applying it, regardless of the fit. On the surface, it looks like you're doing something, but it's not effective. That's why the type of data you collect is crucial. You need to see the whole story as it relates to your particular company. You need to understand how your company is doing in terms of recruiting and retaining a diversity of candidates in real time. In the next chapter, I will share with you what data to collect, where to get it, and what specifically to look for once you have it.

The other half of this framework is retention. In the simplest terms, this is inclusion. Ask yourself four questions about the employees of your company:

1. Who stays?
2. How long do they stay?

3. Do they get promoted? (And, how long does it take to get promoted?)
4. What are you doing to keep them?

The first three questions are answered with the CAPE process, which I will cover in Chapters 3 through 7.

The fourth question; What are you doing to keep them? Is the work you do to develop employee resource groups (ERGs), DE&I training, workshops, and professional development. (I'll cover these in Part II.) Professional development doesn't mean preparing People of Color and women for leadership positions. If this was your first thought, please check your bias now. One of the assumptions that limits opportunities for women and People of Color is that they are unprepared and/or need preparation. Professional development includes the unconscious bias training that all leaders should participate in to reduce bias in the hiring and promotion process.

Key Points

- To change the culture of the organization, you need a shared language and understanding of where the company is going.
- Diversity is about reflecting the mixture of differences and similarities that we find in the world and acknowledging the related tension as we strive to develop more inclusive and high-performing environments.
- Equity is the principle of creating full access and removing barriers to participation. Equity is fair treatment, access, opportunity, and advancement for all people, while at the same time striving to identify and eliminate barriers that prevent the full participation of some groups.
- Inclusion is about making people feel welcomed and valued. Inclusion is retention.
- The best way to get organizational change and create an inclusive environment is to use organizational change models and principles, such as the ADKAR model.

Notes

1. Edward H. Chang and his colleagues (July 9, 2019) wrote a piece in the *Harvard Business Review* entitled "Does diversity training work the way it's supposed to?" Noting that although virtually all Fortune 500 companies offer diversity training of some kind, few of the companies measured the impact of the training. The authors created their own training and tracked outcomes. Findings are intriguing and indicate impact on attitudes but not behaviors. Accessed on April 8, 2021 at https://hbr.org/2019/07/does-diversity-training-work-the-way-its-supposed-to

2. Tyler Sonnemaker (December 31, 2020) summarized the discrimination law suits in 2020 for *Insider*. The article, entitled "2020 brought a wave of discrimination and harassment allegations against major companies, like Amazon, MacDonald's, and Pinterest," noted that 99% of Fortune 500 companies settled at least one discrimination suit since 2000. Accessed on April 8, 2021 at https://www.businessinsider.com/every-company-that-was-sued-discrimination-and-harassment-lawsuits-2020-2021-1

3. The change management process can be a key contributor to the success of your DE&I programs. I've found ADKAR to be helpful. The ADKAR model was created by Prosci founder, Jeff Hiatt. You can find more information about the model, change management, and training opportunities on their website at https://www.prosci.com/methodology/adkar

Chapter 3

Data for DE&I

Fill the Cup of Others

The horrifying images of the attack on our US Capitol on January 6, 2021, left me feeling hopeless. Like many of you, I had a pit in my stomach afterward. Piled on top of the weight of the pandemic and the events after George Floyd's killing, so much violence and hate was too much. I felt numb and empty. I also began to lament if we as a nation were failing our children through our inability to disagree while remaining civil. These thoughts only deepened my sense of emptiness.

The hopelessness I was feeling was compounded by several requests I received from individuals who had asked me to write something they could share through their DE&I departments. The leadership at these companies wanted to help their colleagues with a message to validate the uneasiness we were all feeling while setting a vision for the way forward. My first thought was, "How do I do that? My cup is empty." Typically, writing a response comes easily to me, but this time, the process of trying to write something was surprisingly difficult. My sense of hopelessness was becoming overwhelming.

Then I realized that when my cup feels empty is when I should use whatever drops of hope are left to fill the cups of others. Emptiness is contagious, but so is hopefulness. It is in moments like these when we must live our values.

I had a similar feeling of emptiness after the events of 9/11. What I saw on TV that day was unimaginable. At that time, it seemed we would never recover. We recovered, and we did it by filling the cup of our friends, family, loved ones and colleagues. We reached out to each other when it seemed we had nothing left. It is the act of selflessly giving to others in need, even when it appears that we have nothing left, that defines hope.

Our Union has never been perfect. The attack on our Capitol on January 6, 2021, may have been a new low, but the truth is, that for as much as I love the USA, we have a long history of failures. We were founded on the principles of democracy, but our treatment of Indigenous people, slavery, Jim Crow laws, and the denial of voting rights for women and People of Color are just a few of our many failures as a republic. At the end of the day, our democracy is not and will not be measured by our failures, but how we respond to our failures. Most importantly, each of us as individuals must begin to use our strength to help fill the cups of others.

As a nation, we are at our best when we choose to help our fellow humans in the moments when all seems lost. Throughout our history, the words of many leaders have helped us keep our faith, but it is the individual acts of each of us that make true change. Our humanity lives within each of us and our imperfect Union thrives because each of us uses that humanity.

It was fitting that the week after the January 6 attack we honored Dr. Martin Luther King Jr. As he once said, "An individual has not started living until [they] can rise above the narrow confines of his [their] individualistic concerns to the broader concerns of all humanity." The task for us is to value our humanity more than our desire to be right.

In those moments when our cup feels empty, we must walk in the direction of our moral compass. We must use what little we have to help lift one another up. Remember, hopelessness can be as much of an illusion as being overly optimistic; it all depends on how you look at the world or interpret data.

The Illusion and Challenge of Data

The data on diversity has not been great. Much of the work at some of the largest and best-resourced companies begs for improvement. Some might even argue that DE&I doesn't work at all. We cannot allow that to let us become hopeless. We need to use the data to find solutions, but I have a warning: the data can be an illusion of success or failure. It can be challenging to understand it. The data and your past experiences reflect things that have already happened and cannot be changed. Therefore, you must look forward, even when using data that tells the story of the past. What you do with that information makes the change.

One thing I have learned over the years from talking to many DE&I professionals is that many don't know what data to collect or why they are collecting it. Additionally, even fewer know what affirmative action is or how it works. Without going into detail, affirmative action does not force you to hire X number of African Americans or women. Despite what rumors you have heard or seen on TV, it is not a quota system. On a very basic level, it makes companies collect data on race, ethnicity, gender, and military service.

In 2007, I was tasked with converting Integris Health into an affirmative action employer. At the time, the organization was Oklahoma's largest nonprofit hospital system and had about 10,000 employees. The hospital's leadership had decided to take federal contracts and had recruited a very successful physician who had many research grants. This change made Integris Health a federal contractor, and all federal contractors have to have an affirmative action plan.

At that time, we developed 15 affirmative action plans, and in the process, I realized how much data on race, ethnicity, gender, and military veteran status was being collected. Although I had worked at affirmative action–compliant employers prior to this time, I had never been responsible for developing the plan. This challenge is quite typical for diversity professionals. One of my clients, who was recently promoted to be the chief diversity officer for an employer with over 8,500 employees, confided in me that they did not know how to interpret the affirmative action plan or the data in it, and did not know what demographic data was required.

Generally, most companies have some simple data that show how many minorities currently work for the company or the number of women employed at the company at a certain point in time. Generic data that do not take into account all the variables and barriers to inclusion will have very limited use. Generic data can't tell you if you have recruitment or retention issues or where those issues exist in the company, specifically.

Most companies have oversimplified data, like what is shown in Figure 3.1, which highlights data from Apple, Facebook, Google, Microsoft, and Twitter. This type of data can be misleading and can make the company look more diverse than it is or hide where you need to focus your work.

In Figure 3.1, you can see the percentage of Black (African American) workers in some of the largest tech companies. At first glance it appears that, although all the companies have a relatively low percentage of Black workers, Apple is doing better than its peers.[1] However, the additional information you will need as a DE&I professional will answer questions like *Are the Black workers in leadership positions?* Figure 3.2 represents a portion of Apple's diversity report in July, 2017 that revealed a different view of the same time period.[2]

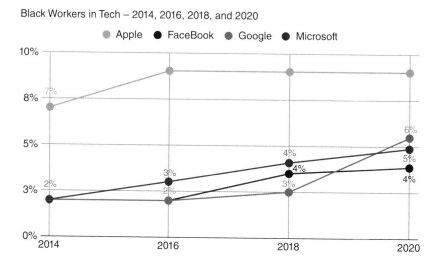

Figure 3.1 Black Workers in Big Tech.
Source: Adapted from Rooney & Khorram, 2020.

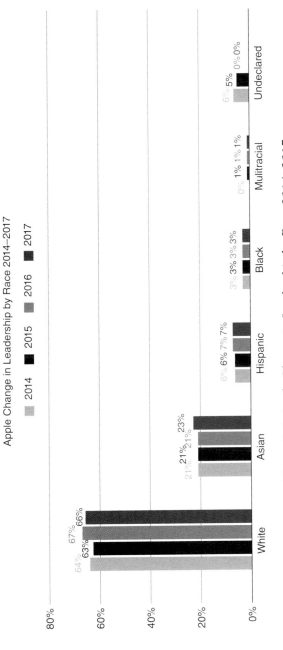

Figure 3.2 Apple Change in Leadership by Race 2014–2017.

If you look closely at the report, you can see that during the period from 2014 to 2017, when Apple was reporting about 8% of their workers were Black, there was no change in the percentage of Blacks in leadership positions.[3] So if you were to just look at the overall diversity of Apple, they looked to be more diverse than their peers, but all the while there was no growth in the number of African American leaders. I would suggest their success was an illusion.

To further illustrate this point, diversity reports may overlook the competing interests and barriers to becoming more diverse. For example, every company has a goal of keeping good people. In fact, many large companies have staff that provide leadership training, and part of that training is designed to teach leaders to manage people with the stated goal of employee retention. If a company is successful in retaining employees, it limits the company's ability to become more diverse because you need people to leave to accomplish that. The simple fact is, no company wants high turnover. Nevertheless, in many cases the only way to meet aggressive diversity goals would be to have high turnover.

While working at the USOPC, I found myself in this situation. The head of human resources at that time was insistent that the company would be 30% diverse in three years, and we should set that as a goal. I kept telling her the goal was not possible as the company only had 10% turnover. She was so insistent that I had to build a spreadsheet to show her the number would be almost impossible to achieve. It is imperative that you be able to explain the realities of how to set expectations to your leadership team, or you are being set up to fail.

In the simplest terms, what I had to explain to my manager was the USOPC had on average 10% turnover and rarely added jobs. This means about 40 of the 400 employees left each year. The USOPC employed approximately 80 POC or (20%). If you want to be at 30% (as she did), the organization would need to go from 80 POC to 120. That would require over a three-year period that at least 50% of all new hires would need to be People of Color (keep in mind that POC only make up about 40% of the population), and we would need to reduce turnover of POCs to 5% or less.

The Recruitment Data Challenge

Remember, the goal for any diversity program is twofold: recruitment and retention. There is a natural tension between these two goals when it comes to employees. (It's not an issue when it comes to customers.) High turnover means inclusion and equity have to be a priority because people are leaving at too high a rate. In other words, an increase in the hiring of People of Color can come about because your inclusion and equity initiatives are not working, and you are adding new POC who simply don't stay.

Conversely, if people are staying at the company longer, inclusion is working, and no one is leaving. When people don't leave, you can't make the company more diverse. There are just not enough opportunities to hire more People of Color, women, persons with disabilities, and so on. Therefore, the diversity of the company grows at a slow rate because any increase in diversity requires people to leave. Even if the company is growing and adding positions, the low turnover can keep the overall diversity of the company low.

The unintended consequence of lower turnover can be a decrease in the number of open positions into which individuals from underrepresented groups can be hired. This would be a good time to consider whether when reporting diversity, you should use a percentage or the real number. Consider the data shown in Figures 3.3 and 3.4.

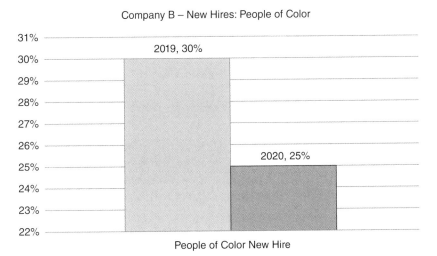

Figure 3.3 Percentage of New Hires: People of Color 2019–2020.

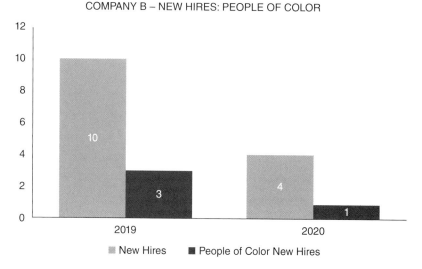

Figure 3.4 Numbers of New Hires: People of Color.

Company B below showed:

• 30% of new hires were People of Color in 2019.
• 25% of new hires were People of Color in 2020.

The data in Figure 3.3 make it look like a decrease in the recruit-ment of employees of Color. Presenting the same data as numbers and not percentages, as in Figure 3.4, tells a different story.

• 3 out of 10 of new hires were People of Color in 2019.
• 1 out of 4 of new hires were People of Color in 2020.

Although this is very small sample, it is a report much like what many leadership teams might see at small companies. So, one year, there is high turnover. In response, you developed a plan to reduce turnover, and it was very effective. The company was good at low-ering turnover, but using a percentage makes it look like your recruit-ment efforts are not working because the percentage of new hires has decreased from 30% to 25%, which is not a great reflection of the work being done. In addition, small numbers can have significant swings.

Using both figures as examples, if they had hired one more Person of Color in 2020, it would make the percentage jump to 50%. Although, in fact, they would have hired one *less* Person of Color in 2020 than they had in 2019.

It all starts with data. That's why the principles of this book are crucial. The way you understand your DE&I data and how you present the data can be paramount in whether the DE&I program is a success or a failure.

I will give more examples as we go along that will show you how to separate theory from practice. At the end of the day, you have to be able to show you know how to run a diversity practice for any size organization.

When trying to improve diversity, equity, and inclusion in the workplace, remember it is not a destination. You will not check the box and be done. Creating a diverse, equitable, and inclusive workplace requires a commitment to the process. It's a journey. To be successful, you will need to have ongoing DE&I training as well as recruitment and retention processes and policies to limit bias. The challenge of data is to understand it and to present it so that it reflects your work.

I will use Chapters 4, 5, 6, and 7 to show you how to apply each step of CAPE and why it works. It's important to understand each component and know how they work together.

KEY POINTS

- Generic data that do not take into account all the variables and barriers to inclusion can't tell you if you have recruitment or retention issues or where those issues exist in the company, specifically.
- If a company is successful in retaining employees, it limits the company's ability to become more diverse. No company wants high employee turnover, so it's important to set realistic expectations for recruitment-based diversity goals.
- Understanding and presenting your diversity data is a key skill for you to have when leading a DE&I program.

Notes

1. Upon the release of Apple's new diversity report, Tony Romm and Rani Molla (November 9, 2017) noted in the title of the article, "Apple is hiring more diverse workers, but its share of women and minorities aren't budging much." Accessed on April 8, 2021 at https://www.vox .com/2017/11/9/16628286/apple-2017-diversity-report-black-asian-white-latino-women-minority

2. Tony Romm and Rani Molla (November 9, 2017) point out that Apple's diversity report showed little change in diversity at the leadership level, in the article entitled "Apple is hiring more diverse workers, but its share of women and minorities aren't budging much." Accessed on April 8, 2021 at https://www.vox.com/2017/11/9/16628286/apple-2017-diversity-report-black-asian-white-latino-women-minority

3. Kate Rooney and Yasmin Khorram (June 12, 2020) reported for CNBC that diversity in tech companies was mostly an annual exercise in publishing the expected diversity reports. Entitled "Tech companies say they value diversity, but reports show little change in the last six years," data show that techs were making very little progress, particularly in hiring Black employees. Accessed on April 8, 2021 at https://www.cnbc.com/2020/06/12/six-years-into-diversity-reports-big-tech-has-made-little-progress.html

Chapter 4

Collect the Data

Give a Brown Guy a Chance

Years ago, when my son, Justus, was about seven, I sat down next to him to watch cartoons. Justus had been sitting there for a little while before I joined him on the couch. After a few minutes of watching, I realized we were watching He-Man. He-Man is a show about a fictional superhero, similar to Superman or Batman.

I had heard of He-Man before but had never really watched the cartoon. The storyline was like most superhero cartoons. He-Man fought against evil and saved people. About halfway through the episode (and during the commercial), I decided to tease Justus. I told Justus, "He-Man is not a real superhero. When I was a kid, we had real superheroes like Superman. He-Man can't even fly!" Like a typical seven-year-old, Justus decided to defend his superhero.

Justus sat up, looked me in the eye, and said, "He-Man is a real superhero; he is strong, he cares, and he helps people!" Then his face turned somewhat sad. He looked down at the ground as if in deep thought and took a deep breath. Justus looked at me with the most introspective face I have ever seen on a seven-year-old. He said,

"I just wish they would give a brown guy a chance." There are few, if any, brown or female superheroes in cartoons.

Justus's simple statement highlighted the importance of our diversity, equity, and inclusion work. I am sure Justus did not want people to take away He-Man; he just wanted to see a superhero that looked like him. DE&I programs are about creating an organization that reflects the diversity we see in the world and the way we know if we reflect that diversity is by collecting data. This is the first step of the CAPE process.

When to Start Collecting Data

If you are starting a new DE&I program (or leading an existing one), I recommend that on day one you start by working on collecting the necessary data about race, ethnicity, gender, military status, and so on. It is harder to get demographic data on employees than one might think, not because the company doesn't have it, but because the process to get the data can be complicated and political. This is something I learned the hard way. I remember the first time I had to present to the board at USOPC I needed demographic data for a table. I requested the information weeks in advance, and I got the data at the close of business the day before the presentation. It took a long time to get the data partly because the head of HR at that time had an attitude that was less than supportive toward the new DE&I program and partly because the person that compiled the data was overwhelmed with other work. As I mentioned, DE&I is about relationships, and early on, I had not yet developed any.

> **JASON-ISM**
> In DE&I, it all starts with data.

I stayed up all night building the tables. Remember, having the data and having it in a table to present are two different things. I also found out that the size of the company doesn't; it always takes a long time to get the data. I have worked in companies with over 8,500 employees and at USOPC that only had about 400 employees at that time; it still took forever to get employee data. There are several reasons for this: sometimes they simply don't collect diversity data, or the data is not in the format or table needed, so it has to be built either by you or the data manager. Another major factor is there could be several other projects ahead of yours. So be sure to ask for the diversity data as soon as you can because you need to be in the queue.

The collection of data is going to be fundamental for any diversity program. I strongly encourage you to launch the diversity program with data collection. If you are in an existing DE&I program, you still need to make sure you have access to the necessary demographic data. We will talk more about the other components of launching/running a DE&I program, and we will get specific about the how-tos. But for now, I want to start with data because this will be a fundamental piece in identifying problems, prioritizing your work, and measuring outcomes.

What Data to Collect

The first question most diversity officers ask is always *What specific demographic data do I need to collect?* By demographic data, I am referring to race, ethnicity, age, sex, LGBTQ+, gender, persons with disabilities, and military veterans. You will also want hire and termination dates, promotions, titles, departments, and tenure. Not all companies collect data in all of these categories, but you need to know which ones are being collected and which ones can be added. Don't assume your company is already collecting all the data that is necessary to build an effective and inclusive DE&I plan.

The second thing you need to know is when in the recruitment process, data like race, ethnicity, gender, LGBTQ+, etc. are collected?

It is important to know exactly when in the employee life cycle the demographic data is being collected. Where do the data points come from? Is the company collecting the data during the application process? Or are they collecting the data after hire? Ideally, you should collect demographic data at both points, but not all companies do both things. You will also want to periodically resurvey your current employees.

Many companies only collect data at hire. If that is the case, there is no way to measure or track the diversity of candidates who apply. This is very important data to collect because it is the best measure of your recruitment efforts. Your company may have little diversity because you have hiring bias, meaning the applicant pool is diverse but applicants from underrepresented groups are never selected for the opportunity. This would necessitate a different solution as you would need to work with hiring managers and not recruiters.

Data collection may seem elementary, but a survey conducted by Affirmity and Human Capital Media Research and Advisory group showed that almost 40% of the companies surveyed "don't know what to measure or why" or "measure everything, but don't know what actions we should be taking" (Figure 4.1)[1]

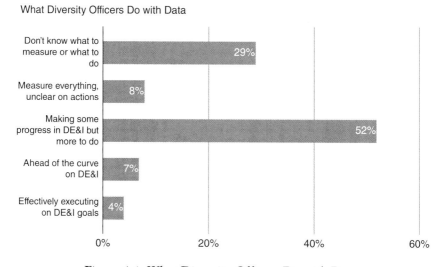

Figure 4.1 What Diversity Officers Do with Data.

Source: Based on the HCM and Affirmity 2019 report on the lessons learned between 2015 and 2019 on strategic diversity measurement, entitled "Moving the needle on strategic diversity." Accessed on April 8, 2021 at https://www.affirmity.com/wp-content/uploads/2019/08/HCM-Workforce-Strategic-Diversity-Measurement-2019-White-Paper.pdf Redrawn from data from Affirmity 2019 White Paper.

Where to Get the Demographic Data You Need

To get started on data collection for your company, I would recommend that you get a copy of your company's EEO-1 form.[2] The EEO-1 form is a survey overseen by the Equal Employment Opportunity Commission (Figure 4.2). Most companies with over fifty employees submit this

Joint Reporting Committee
- Equal Employment Opportunity Commission
- Office of Federal Contract Compliance Programs (Labor)

EQUAL EMPLOYMENT OPPORTUNITY

EMPLOYER INFORMATION REPORT EEO—1

Standard Form 100 (Rev. 3/97)
O.M.B. No. 3046-0007
EXPIRES 10/31/99
100-214

SAMPLE

Section A—TYPE OF REPORT

Refer to instructions for number and types of reports to be filed.

1. Indicate by marking in the appropriate box the type of reporting unit for which this copy of the form is submitted (MARK ONLY ONE BOX).

(1) ☐ Single-establishment Employer Report

Multi-establishment Employer:
(2) ☐ Consolidated Report (Required)
(3) ☐ Headquarters Unit Report (Required)
(4) ☐ Individual Establishment Report (submit one for each establishment with 50 or more employees)
(5) ☐ Special Report

2. Total number of reports being filed by this Company (Answer on Consolidated Report only) ______

Section B—COMPANY IDENTIFICATION *(To be answered by all employers)* — OFFICE USE ONLY

1. Parent Company
   a. Name of parent company (owns or controls establishment in item 2) omit if same as label — a.

Address (Number and street) — b.

City or town | State | ZIP code — c.

2. Establishment for which this report is filed. (Omit if same as label)
   a. Name of establishment — d.

Address (Number and street) | City or Town | County | State | ZIP code — e.

   b. Employer Identification No. (IRS 9-DIGIT TAX NUMBER) — f.

   c. Was an EEO–1 report filed for this establishment last year? ☐ Yes ☐ No

Section C—EMPLOYERS WHO ARE REQUIRED TO FILE *(To be answered by all employers)*

☐ Yes ☐ No 1. Does the entire company have at least 100 employees in the payroll period for which you are reporting?

☐ Yes ☐ No 2. Is your company affiliated through common ownership and/or centralized management with other entities in an enterprise with a total employment of 100 or more?

☐ Yes ☐ No 3. Does the company or any of its establishments (a) have 50 or more employees AND (b) is not exempt as provided by 41 CFR 60–1.5, AND either (1) is a prime government contractor or first-tier subcontractor, and has a contract, subcontract, or purchase order amounting to $50,000 or more, or (2) serves as a depository of Government funds in any amount or is a financial institution which is an issuing and paying agent for U.S. Savings Bonds and Savings Notes?

If the response to question C–3 is yes, please enter your Dun and Bradstreet identification number (if you have one):

NOTE: If the answer is yes to questions 1, 2, or 3, complete the entire form, otherwise skip to Section G.

Figure 4.2 Sample EEO-1 Form.

Source: Employer Information Report, EEO-1.

BF 100 Page 2

Section D—EMPLOYMENT DATA

Employment at this establishment—Report all permanent full-time and part-time employees including apprentices and on-the-job trainees unless specifically excluded as set forth in the instructions. Enter the appropriate figures on all lines and in all columns. Blank spaces will be considered as zeros.

JOB CATEGORIES		OVERALL TOTALS (SUM OF COL. B THRU K)	NUMBER OF EMPLOYEES									
			MALE					FEMALE				
			WHITE (NOT OF HISPANIC ORIGIN)	BLACK (NOT OF HISPANIC ORIGIN)	HISPANIC	ASIAN OR PACIFIC ISLANDER	AMERICAN INDIAN OR ALASKAN NATIVE	WHITE (NOT OF HISPANIC ORIGIN)	BLACK (NOT OF HISPANIC ORIGIN)	HISPANIC	ASIAN OR PACIFIC ISLANDER	AMERICAN INDIAN OR ALASKAN NATIVE
		A	B	C	D	E	F	G	H	I	J	K
Officials and Managers	1											
Professionals	2											
Technicians	3											
Sales Workers	4											
Office and Clerical	5											
Craft Workers (Skilled)	6											
Operatives (Semi-Skilled)	7											
Laborers (Unskilled)	8											
Service Workers	9											
TOTAL	10											
Total employment reported in previous EEO-1 report	11											

NOTE: Omit questions 1 and 2 on the Consolidated Report.
1. Date(s) of payroll period used: _____   2. Does this establishment employ apprentices?   1 ☐ Yes   2 ☐ No

Section E—ESTABLISHMENT INFORMATION (Omit on the Consolidated Report)

1. What is the major activity of this establishment? (Be specific, i.e., manufacturing steel castings, retail grocer, wholesale plumbing supplies, title insurance, etc. Include the specific type of product or type of service provided, as well as the principal business or industrial activity.)

OFFICE USE ONLY

Section F—REMARKS

Use this item to give any identification data appearing on last report which differs from that given above, explain major changes in composition of reporting units and other pertinent information.

Section G—CERTIFICATION (See Instructions G)

Check one
1 ☐ All reports are accurate and were prepared in accordance with the instructions (check on consolidated only)
2 ☐ This report is accurate and was prepared in accordance with the instructions.

Name of Certifying Official	Title	Signature	Date
Name of person to contact regarding this report (Type or print)	Address (Number and Street)		
Title	City and State	ZIP Code	Telephone Number (Including Area Code)	Extension

All reports and information obtained from individual reports will be kept confidential as required by Section 709(e) of Title VII. WILLFULLY FALSE STATEMENTS ON THIS REPORT ARE PUNISHABLE BY LAW, U.S. CODE, TITLE 18, SECTION 1001.

Figure 4.2 (*Continued*)

form by May 1 of every year. It requires employment data to be categorized by race/ethnicity, gender, and job category.

Getting a copy of the EEO-1 is a great starting point and will give you a quick snapshot of the company's diversity. Depending on when you get a copy of the EEO-1, it may be outdated, but there are several things you can learn from it that will be very helpful to you. First, you will see that all of the employees are put into about nine job categories, such as professionals or skilled craft workers. Not every company uses all of the categories. So you may have fewer job categories on your company's EEO-1 than you see in Figure 4.2. Nonetheless, the EEO-1 is an essential piece of data you need to collect.

Second, you will quickly be able to see if there is a glass ceiling in the company. Are all the women at or below the manager level? Are the People of Color at or below the director level? This is a simple data point you can use to build your program. We will cover more in Chapters 5 and 6, but you now have a way to track the effectiveness of your DE&I work. You can say, "We started on X date when we identified a glass ceiling and put in a program/initiative and after one year saw an increase in the number of women and People of Color in leadership positions." That is a specific and measurable goal. When you look at the company's EEO-1, you will be able to quickly identify a few areas for your attention (which we will talk more about in the next chapter).

The other places where you will find company employee demographic data is in the applicant tracking system (ATS) and the human resource information system (HRIS). It is important that you understand the difference between ATS and HRIS and what data is available from each system.

The ATS is where the data, taken at the application phase, is kept. It helps the recruiters and hiring managers keep track of job candidates. This is where information, like resumés, tracking job applicants, matching candidates with open positions, and scheduling interviews is kept. The HRIS system is where information about benefits, payroll processes, time and attendance, sick leave, vacation time, and performance management is kept. Essentially, ATS is where the data about those that applied for jobs can be found. HRIS is where information about current or past employees is located. Sometimes they are connected, sometimes they are all in one system, and sometimes they don't work together very well.

There are some companies that use one system for both processes, but if not, you'll need to have a general understanding of both the ATS and HRIS systems to start your DE&I plan. If you find demographic data is not in the ATS system, it may not be surprising. Not all companies collect demographic data at the application point. So, I would strongly encourage you to begin collecting demographic information at this point if your company is not already doing so. Otherwise, it's a missed opportunity to better understand and have an impact on the DE&I goals of your company.

It's important that you get the right information from the beginning, so you need to understand where the data you need is kept and that it is collected on an ongoing basis. You will be accessing this data on a regular basis. It's going to be of paramount importance to you later, and so I would strongly encourage you to make sure early on that you start collecting everything you need.

Who Is Being Included in the Data?

In some cases, the collection of demographic data is done when the application is submitted, but it doesn't include information on persons with disabilities. A surprising number of companies don't collect information on disabilities. The assumption behind this data omission is that if we don't collect data about individuals with disabilities, we cannot be accused of discrimination because we did not know the person had a disability.

It's a false assumption, and there is no excuse for not collecting this data. I would point out that even if a person with a disability did accuse the company of discrimination, it is fundamentally bigoted to attach a concern of potential litigation to every person with a disability. Also, any discrimination claim should be investigated and changes made accordingly. Furthermore, avoiding a potential discrimination claim by professing ignorance does nothing to further your DE&I efforts on behalf of the company.

This kind of "ignorance-is-bliss" reaction from the company does not create an atmosphere of inclusion and certainly does not improve your company's diversity. We also know, historically, that persons with disabilities in the United States have some of the highest unemployment rates, and it is these kinds of discriminatory practices that have contributed to this form of systemic marginalization.

This is something that can and should be changed. I would also suggest you take some time to investigate what process your company uses for a candidate to inform the company that they need an accommodation for the interview, as well as for employment once hired.

You will want to know how many applicants were in each category and, then, how many of those applicants were interviewed and subsequently hired. As I stated above, you may find out that there are plenty of diverse applicants but very few are interviewed and fewer are hired. As a DE&I officer, data can show you where the problem begins.

It's Also About Who Is Not in the Room

Regardless of the size of your company, you can still collect data around diversity, equity, and inclusion and analyze that data so it serves your company. Data can be collected anywhere from employees to customers. Here is an example: you've started collecting data and discover that women hate your product, but men love it. You look around the office and there are six guys in your company and no women; that might explain the data. That's the analyze part.

Looking at who is not in the room, and who is not consuming your product would be a huge opportunity for company growth.

Respecting Demographic Data

Keep in mind that information about individuals that are members of the LGBTQ+ community may not be available. In many cases, companies did not ask because prior to the Supreme Court decision in 2020,[3] LGBTQ+ was not a protected class in all states. Therefore, most companies never collected this data.

The difficult thing is that you may find that a lot of people choose not to share this information. This hesitancy may diminish over time as they go from being recruited to being retained. If they feel that your company is serious about diversity, they may decide at a later date to disclose their demographic information. Also, it is possible that a person did not have a disability when hired and, due to unforeseen circumstances, became a person with a disability while employed. You would want to capture that change in diversity status for your company.

Be sensitive to your employees' rights to privacy and protection from discrimination. It is appropriate to ask for all the needed demographic information, but you need to protect the integrity of the data by limiting access to the information. I also recommend using an asterisk in any table or graph if there are fewer than five individuals in a certain category or department so that you can protect their identities.

If you are the type of employer that embraces diversity, employees will feel safe checking the boxes that indicate who they are and how they identify. It's okay to ask people more than once.

One of the things you will find if you start reporting demographic data is that people will start questioning the numbers. I led the transition for both Techstars (a company with about 400 employees at that time) and INTEGRIS (close to 10,000 employees) in becoming affirmative action employers. One of my most vivid memories from both companies is hearing things like, "Well, I know our company is more diverse than what we find in our data. Can I put their demographic information in for them?" I would strongly discourage you from doing that as everyone has a right to identify themself and/or can choose not to share it.

Remember, the information that is given to you is typically outdated the moment you get it because many companies onboard new employees and have people leave on a daily or weekly basis. I would strongly encourage you to know on what date the information was compiled and use similar if not the same date to compile and prepare the report. You will want to do this year-over-year or quarterly as a way to measure progress.

Collecting the demographic data to use as the foundation of your DE&I program will create a work environment that reflects the diversity we see in the world.

KEY POINTS

- It is harder to get demographic data on employees than one might think, not because the company doesn't have it, but because the process to get the data can be complicated and political.
- Collect data related to employee and applicant race, ethnicity, age, sex, LGBTQ+, gender, persons with disabilities, and military veteran status. You will also want hire and termination dates, promotions, titles, departments, and tenure.
- Many companies only collect data at the time of hire. If that is the case, there is no way to measure or track the diversity of candidates who apply.
- Be sensitive to your employees' rights to privacy and protection from discrimination. It is appropriate to ask for all the needed demographic information, but you need to protect the integrity of the data by limiting access to the information.

Notes

1. Affirmity partnered with the Human Capital Research and Advisory Group to produce a report, released in 2019, on the lessons learned between 2015 and 2019 on strategic diversity measurement, entitled "Moving the needle on strategic diversity." The report was based on a survey conducted in 2019 and indicated, among other findings, that progress falls along a continuum with some companies clearly out-in-front with advanced practices in D&I. Accessed on April 8, 2021 at https://www.affirmity.com/wp-content/uploads/2019/08/HCM-Workforce-Strategic-Diversity-Measurement-2019-White-Paper.pdf
2. The EEO-1 report information is publicly available and downloadable from the website of the Equal Employment Opportunity Commission. Accessed on April 8, 2021 at https://eeocdata.org/eeo1 Instructions and resources are also available, such as an FAQ at https://eeocdata.org/eeo1/support/faq
3. In October 2019, in Bostock v. Clayton County, Georgia, the Supreme Court held that employers are violating Title VII if they fire an employee for being gay or transgender. Accessed on April 8, 2021 at https://www.supremecourt.gov/opinions/19pdf/17-1618_hfci.pdf

Chapter 5

Analyze the Data

Seeing It So Clear Now

"Babylon" is a song written and performed by David Gray. It is one of my favorite songs, and I have found that the melody always relaxes me. In the lyrics of the song, Gray sings about a moment of clarity in feeling unafraid of admitting mistakes.

I recently heard an interview with David Gray. He talked about the moment and the context in which he wrote "Babylon." He said he was in a small second-floor apartment on a perfect summer afternoon. The sun was up. He had the apartment windows open, and a perfect breeze was coming through the window. He could hear the street noise, and it was comforting. He could hear the cars passing, but it was the kind of traffic you hear on a Sunday afternoon when people are driving but not on their way to work. The birds were chirping, and it was the perfect temperature with the kind of breeze that cools the skin but doesn't knock anything off the table.

In that environment Gray was able to sit down with his guitar and write, arguably, the best song of his career. He said during the interview he knew the song was good, but he did not know how good.

Gray said, "I didn't know what I had." It was clear from the interview that hindsight had provided him with the vision to see things clearly, as he described in the song. "Babylon" turned out to be a great song, far beyond anything Gray had imagined.

Several years ago, when my son, Justus, was close to graduation from high school, I was reminded of the lyrics above and came to the realization that, like the narrator in "Babylon," I didn't truly know what I had. Justus is the best son that I could have ever asked for in life. He continues to think more of me than I deserve and continues to amaze me with his desire to please others.

The year Justus was a senior in high school was the most difficult of my life, and I often found myself on the verge of tears. The thought of him graduating from high school and starting the next chapter of his life came with mixed emotions of pride, happiness, and sadness. I was going to miss him, and I simply did not know how everything would turn out.

I wish I had recognized what I had and enjoyed him more while he was growing up. I know sometimes my words hurt him more than I had intended. I often wish I could take back all the hurtful words. As a parent, one tries so hard to keep your kids from hurt and make sure they are ready for the world. Sometimes in that process I spent too much time worried about Justus's eating with his mouth open or trying to make sure he had good manners. If I had known what I had in Justus and how fast high school goes by, I would have enjoyed my time with him more.

Justus went on to college and did very well for himself and continues to thrive. I still wish I had spent more time simply enjoying him. I wish I had spent more time enjoying being a dad to both my kids. At the end of the day, being a father and having Justus as a son and Piper as a daughter was far better than anything I could have imagined.

In life you need to know what you have, and in DE&I work, collecting the data is one of the ways we know what we have.

Using the Data to Know What You Have

In the Chapters 2 and 3, we covered what, when, who, and how to collect the data, which brings us to the next CAPE step: Analyze the data. What do I mean by that? Simple. You analyze the data you collected to find the patterns because you need to know what you have in the context of DE&I.

Given what you've heard or already know about the company and looking at what the data show, does the company think it is diverse because of gender but has very little racial diversity? Or, are all entry-level positions diverse, but there is no diversity in the leadership positions? These are some of the patterns you need to be looking for in your company. Many times, the human resources department tends to be much more gender diverse than accounting, or the accounting department tends to be less racially diverse than the marketing department. Analyze what you have from all angles and levels. There are trends you will want to identify in order to maximize your time, make the best use of your resources, and create targeted DE&I plans, initiatives, and solutions.

When you analyze the data, you may miss the true picture if you only look at the company in its entirety. For example, if your marketing department has high gender diversity, and the accounting department does too, but the engineering department does not, you may believe that your company is diverse overall. As an example, refer to Figure 5.1.

You will not able to see the lack of gender diversity in the engineering department because the other departments have such high gender diversity. By isolating the engineering department, you will have identified an area of focus. In this example, the company is

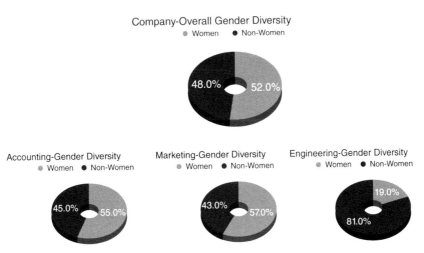

Figure 5.1 Gender Diversity Overall and by Department.

reporting 52% gender diversity. That will generally sound good, but the engineering department is only 19% gender diverse. What is happening is that the higher gender diversity percentages in the marketing and accounting departments pull up the company average.

The 19% gender diversity in the engineering department is a very interesting number. The number will need to be put into context. You need to know if 19% is high or low as compared to the number of women engineers available. For example, about 40% of all chemical engineers are women, whereas only about 17.2% of civil engineers are women. Therefore, if your company employs civil engineers, 19% would be above average. If your company employs chemical engineers, you need a plan to recruit more women engineers because you are quite low compared to the profession as a whole. This is not to say you can't set a higher expectation, but it has to be a realistic expectation. A goal of 40% women civil engineers would not be realistic, as it would require you to hire women at a rate that would be twice their availability in the market, and you would need high turnover in the engineering department to make those hires.

Understanding how to analyze the data will give you a way forward. You can build a plan with a strategy and measurable outcomes. You can say, "I've analyzed this data, and I know I need to increase gender diversity in the engineering department but not necessarily across the board." If you don't break down the data by department, you may feel overwhelmed when pressed with the need to diversify your company. You might feel as though you have to do a company-wide diversity plan, when really, after analyzing the data, it actually tells you how to make your efforts more focused and targeted on one department, a focus that is much more manageable. This way, you have maximized your time through data analysis. You have a strategy that you can execute, and you know where to focus your effort for success.

Generally speaking, diversity departments are underfunded and understaffed. This means it's incredibly important to simplify the process and maximize your resources. Tailor the plan to your company's specific needs with the resources you have at your disposal. That will prove to be the best use of your time.

Over the last 15 years, I have launched four different DE&I programs in four different industries. Every time, I try to build a diversity program that is unique to the organization. There is one constant across all four of the companies that I launched programs for: There was no budget and no staff. I have never started with more than $50,000, and I have never had any staff on the day I started. How did the data help me? Because if you have no staff and very limited budget, you need to be efficient and maximize resources.

I can vividly remember starting at INTEGRIS Health as the new vice president for diversity and inclusion. It was my first executive position, my first time starting a diversity program, and I was all by myself. INTEGRIS was the largest nonprofit hospital system in the state of Oklahoma with about 10,000 employees, and the CEO was Stanley Hupfeld. Hupfeld was an icon in Oklahoma. He had taken quite a risk in creating a DE&I program in 2007 because there were not a lot of hospitals launching DE&I programs in Oklahoma at the time. In fact, the OU Medical Center, one of the major hospital systems in Oklahoma, didn't hire a diversity officer until 2019.

In 2007, I had not developed the CAPE program; therefore, I was feeling overwhelmed trying to start a DE&I program and did not know where to start. I was going to need a process and a way to show success. With about 10,000 employees and 15 locations, I was thinking, *What do I fix first?* We needed more doctors of Color, we need more nurses of Color, there were patient outcome needs, and I was the only person doing DE&I for a 10,000-person company that had never had a DE&I program. One of the first things I realized was that if everyone has a different view of DE&I and how to define success, I was going to struggle. Moreover, I need to figure out what data I should be tracking to use as a baseline. There were a lot of mistakes and lessons learned at INTERGIS, so trust me, when I tell you the CAPE process works. It can save you a lot of time.

If you don't analyze your data, you don't know where your opportunities or successes can be within the organization. As a result, you typically create a strategy or a program that feels unwieldy, and you, as the diversity officer, become overwhelmed. All you see are the problems, and you don't see where to start or how to affect change. This is where CAPE helps you. The analytical piece is really important because you use the analysis of your data to determine how to make the best use of your time and resources. You don't have unlimited resources, so you need to know what works.

The How: Analyzing Data to Identify Recruitment Issues

I always tell people, that diversity, equity, and inclusion come down to two things – recruitment and retention. Remember that when you look at your data analysis. It will tell you if you need to do recruitment work or if your company would be better served focusing on retention.

Most diversity officers don't have enough bandwidth or budget to implement a recruitment program that would allow you to oversee every single hire. So, by analyzing data, you can decide what's the best use of your time. Typically, most companies don't have a lot of senior-level hires because those jobs don't turn over very often. You will also find that some departments make more hires than others or are much more diverse in their hiring. In your data analysis for recruitment, you are looking for hiring trends, volume of hires, and impact. So, let's take a moment to explain how to do that in the context of recruitment.

For example, if a department has a trend of very few hires of People of Color, this will need your attention. You might need to look at the data concerning the diversity of the pool of applicants (typically found in the ATS system). If you can identify that there were no People of Color in the pool for the hiring manager to select from, training on unconscious bias is not going to be effective. Why? Because the hiring manager never saw a Person of Color to interview or hire. The work needs to be done with the recruiter and recruitment process, not the hiring manager.

Take a close look Figure 5.2. You will notice the diversity of the applicant pool is consistently more diverse than the diversity of those hired. The way to interpret this table is that the recruiters are finding applicants of Color but they are being hired at a rate much lower than their percent of the applicant pool. These data demonstrate that you have selection bias, not a limited applicant pool. This is a good example where unconscious bias training would make sense and be most effective.

Unconscious bias is having a belief system (usually negative) about a person or group of persons despite evidence to the contrary. Since unconscious bias is unconscious, most people aren't aware of their particular biases. And the thing is, everyone has them. By tracking this data, you are tracking what may be unconscious bias.

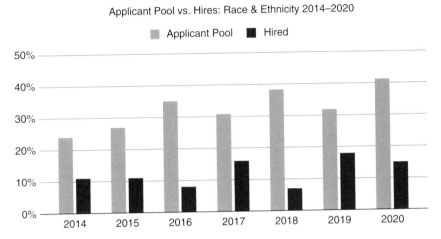

Figure 5.2 Sample Applicant Pool versus Hiring Data.

The next two pieces of the recruitment puzzle are the volume of hires and impact. As I mentioned, some departments make a lot of hires, but that doesn't necessarily mean that these departments would need the majority of your time and attention. When analyzing the data, you may find diverse pools of applicants and a diverse group of hires in a department with a high volume of hires. There would be no reason to spend your time and resources on this department because the diversity volume within the department is not a problem.

However, beware that you don't confuse high volume with impact. I can promise you that all senior-level positions are typically low volume, but they will need your attention because they are high impact. They are high impact because of their visibility, and one of the ways a company's commitment to DE&I is measured is by the diversity of its leadership team. So, be sure to analyze the data to ensure that you are making the right decisions about what you need to do.

The How: Analyzing Data to Identify Retention Issues

Diversity, equity, and inclusion programs must retain good employees. The retention piece means analyzing data that show whether or not individuals from underrepresented groups are being retained and promoted at the same rate as their peers. For example, if you find that a lot of People of Color are in entry-level positions but not in senior leadership positions, you probably have *promotion bias*. Promotion bias occurs when internal candidates are not promoted to senior positions due to unconscious bias. If promotion bias is a problem, you need to address it specifically instead of making broad efforts related to recruitment or retention.

You might also find different forms of bias reflected in how annual reviews are completed, causing high turnover and/or low promotion rates. An article in the *Harvard Business Review* titled "How Gender Bias Corrupts Performance Reviews, and What to Do About It"[1] cited research that showed women were "1.4 times more likely to receive critical subjective feedback (as opposed to either positive feedback or critical objective feedback)." I would encourage you to look at annual reviews of women, People of Color, persons with disabilities, LGBTQ+ employees, and/or other underrepresented groups. You may find they are rated on average much lower than their peers. Comparing promotions and terminations with ratings in annual reviews of underrepresented groups to their peers may explain discrepancies and uncover bias in your annual review process. Generally, if a group of individuals feel the review and promotion process is not equitable, they leave.

Equally important when you analyze the data is the need to identify whether your company has a glass ceiling. Look at the different levels of leadership in the company and see how diverse your leaders and executives are by gender, race, ethnicity, LGBTQ+, and persons with disabilities. This analysis will help you develop a recruitment strategy and plan to help the company identify diverse candidates in the categories that are underrepresented on the leadership team.

By analyzing your data, you will know where to start and what is working. If you find the marketing team has been very successful in recruiting persons with disabilities, perhaps you can borrow from what they are doing in the marketing department. Many times, a best practice may already be working in the company. You will need this data because you want to be able to show wins as well as opportunities to diversify.

If, for example, you find that persons with disabilities never stay in the organization more than one year, you have a retention issue. You know that you don't have selection bias related to hiring. You have something going on in the culture that makes persons with disabilities want to leave, and that needs to be addressed.

JASON-ISM
DE&I training is not a fix in and of itself.

Take the time to look at the retention statistics of individual departments and leaders to ascertain if the problem is with promotion or if there were simply no opportunities to hire. If you understand the data on who's being hired, when they're being hired, in which departments, and how long they stay or get promoted, then you have a better idea of what to do from day-to-day and year-to-year, and determine the best use of your time and resources. In the simplest terms, you are looking for patterns in hiring, retention, promotions, and terminations.

Sometimes the data looks the same two years in a row, and that doesn't necessarily mean that you haven't been successful in increasing diversity. If, for example, in Figure 5.3, you have ten executive leaders, two of whom are women, that translates to 20% gender diversity at the end of 2020. Consider this: If at the end of 2021, you still have ten executive leaders, two of which are women, you would report 20% two years in a row, which might look like failure or that nothing's changed.

But let's assume the only two women executives left during 2020 and you replaced them with two women, your diversity work is actually at 100%. Why? Because when you had two opportunities to hire gender diversity onto the leadership team, you did. The overall gender diversity may remain at 20%, but just because there was no increase doesn't mean your work is 0%. Understanding the data and knowing how to present it, is an essential skill for a successful DE&I officer.

Figure 5.3 Year over Year Recruitment Data by Gender.

I have seen a lot of diversity officers miss an opportunity to highlight their successes. In this example, you had an opportunity to show that you can recruit diverse candidates, and you were able to execute on that objective. Therefore, that 20% may look like failure when, in fact, it could be indicative of an effective DE&I program. You can only make change when you have an opportunity to make change. It is important to be able to present to the CEO, the leadership team, and the board the right data that will more accurately depict your success in your diversity work.

> **JASON-ISM**
> You can only make change when you have an opportunity to make change.

Assume Competence

I am often told we don't have enough women (and in particular, Women of Color) in the pipeline for senior leadership jobs. Here's my take on that: There are enough women (and Women of Color) in the pipeline – if you assume competence.

What do I mean by *assume competence*? Let me give you an example. Women make up 100% of the athletes in women's volleyball in the NCAA.[2] Yet not even 50% of the coaches are women. There were only 22 men's volleyball programs in 2020 at the Division I level in the NCAA, yet they apparently produce enough coaches to supply almost 60% of the coaches for 334 women's Division I programs. By using the NCAA data, I was also able to see that there has only been one female coach of a men's Division I volleyball team between 2012 and 2020. During that same period, there was never a time in which female coaches outnumbered male coaches for women's volleyball teams at the NCAA Division I level. Women have never even made up 50% of the coaches in women's volleyball at the Division I level.

Over 75% of the athletes who play volleyball in the US are women and 100% of the athletes in Division I women's volleyball are women. It would be fair to say that men are underrepresented in women's volleyball, yet there is no pipeline problem of men to coach women's volleyball. To my knowledge, after some brief searching, there are zero programs that prepare men to coach women's volleyball. There is no leaky pipeline study, no *Lean In* book telling men what to do to coach in a female-dominated sport.

Why do we not have a pipeline problem for men coaching women's sports? We assume competence. We assume men who have never played women's volleyball (or other women's sports) can coach women's volleyball. There are key differences in the skills and strategies of men's and women's volleyball. Nonetheless, we assume not only that men's skills at playing men's volleyball are useful and transferable, but also that they can go to any level and coach – lead, instruct, motivate, develop winning strategies for a women's volleyball team, even though they have never played this exact sport.

To put it bluntly, we assume whatever experience a man had before makes him competent to coach women. There is an assumption that a man is fundamentally competent. This simple example reveals a blatant pattern and bias. Men are assumed to be competent to coach women's sports. Now, compare that to women coaching men's sports. The fact that there are almost no women coaching men's sports is a pattern. If the college athletics world assumed women's competence as coaches, there would be many qualified candidates. Take the time to analyze the data and find the patterns.

Using the data you've collected and analyzed to build the DE&I plan is next, in Chapter 6, but all of these examples show you how data and your analysis of it will build a foundation for an effective program. To run an effective DE&I program, you have to identify the best use of your time and resources to put in a DE&I Plan.

KEY POINTS

- Identify trends to maximize your time, make the best use of your resources, and create targeted DE&I solutions.
- Unconscious bias is having a belief system (usually negative) about a person or group of persons despite evidence to the contrary.
- Context is important. You need to know how a department's diversity rate compares to the diversity of the field to ensure alignment between diversity goals and the pool of available applicants.
- There are enough candidates from underrepresented groups in the pipeline – if you assume competence.

Notes

1. Paola Cecchi-Dimeglio (April 12, 2017) wrote a piece for the *Harvard Business Review* entitled "How gender bias corrupts performance reviews, and what to do about it." The author notes that a similar situation will get either a negative or positive interpretation based on gender. Accessed on April 8, 2021 at https://hbr.org/2017/04/how-gender-bias-corrupts-performance-reviews-and-what-to-do-about-it

2. Data come from the NCAA website. There is a program on the website that can be used to analyze the data from their tables. Accessed on April 8, 2021 at https://www.ncaa.org/about/resources/research/ncaa-demographics-database

Chapter 6

Plan your Program

The World's Park

People often ask me, "What is diversity?"

It is a walk in the world's park. I am sure this does not make much sense to you, but it might if you were a three-year-old riding in a stroller.

When my son was three and my daughter was one, we lived one house away from a park. My son, Justus, would beg every day to go for a walk in the park. Most days I would take him, but the walks were very frustrating endeavors. As soon as I would get to the park, Justus would want out of the stroller to look at or touch something. I would unstrap him, and Justus would jump down and look at something and explain to me that I should look too. I would say, "Okay, Justus, I have seen a dandelion before; please get back in the stroller. We are trying to take a walk." Justus would get back in, and three steps later, he would want out again. I would let him out and he would say, "Look, Dad, a butterfly." I would respond with, "Okay, Justus but I have seen a butterfly before. I thought you wanted to take a walk. Please get back in the stroller."

Three more steps and the whole thing started over, but this time it would be a little dog. As you can imagine, these walks took forever in a very small park. Justus would point out everything from a ladybug to the swing set and even some of the neighbors. Justus pointed out some things to me three or four times. Justus could tell by my responses that I was not really taking in the wonder of a dandelion, so he would insist that I look. "See, Dad! This one is different than the last one." I would try to respond in a more animated way to persuade him to get back in the stroller, something like, "Yes, Justus, I do see the dandelion! It is amazing!" Luckily, most three-year-olds don't get sarcasm. I would also remind Justus that we were taking a walk. "I thought you wanted to take a walk, Justus."

Then one day, it dawned on me that Justus was giving me a diversity lesson. The reason you go on a walk is to take in all the beauty around us. One should take time to enjoy the many colors, shapes, people, bugs, and even dandelions. A walk in the park is not a race around the trail; it is not even a walk. It is an opportunity to enjoy the many wonders of the world, including a three-year-old boy giving you a lesson.

Much of the work we do in the area of diversity is the same. By pointing out a cute puppy, we don't detract from the beauty of a butterfly. In fact, sometimes when I see a dandelion, it helps me to appreciate the dandelion-free grass in my backyard. Likewise, understanding and learning to appreciate the culture, views, and/or beliefs of others helps us to appreciate our own culture. Appreciating diversity is an opportunity to learn, grow, and take a walk in the park. Diversity is a strategy to grow your business and develop tomorrow's leaders. Our DE&I work is a journey.

JASON-ISM

DE&I training is part of an ongoing program to move the company culture.

As the chief diversity, equity, and inclusion officer, you are tasked with creating and maintaining an environment in which the uniqueness of every person is embraced – a workplace that reflects the diversity found in the world, where the playing field is level, and where everyone feels respected and valued at work. To do that, you need to come up with a plan.

Plan Only after You Analyze the Data

When you think about CAPE as *collect, analyze, plan,* and *execute,* it sounds a little out of sequence because almost every organization starts with the diversity plan. How often in the context of diversity work have we been told, "You *should* have a diversity plan." I wouldn't tell you *not* to have a diversity plan, but generally what happens when you start with the plan is that you build solutions that are looking for a problem. As a result, what you find is that the plan stops working, it gets stalled, you can't measure your success or failure, and people get frustrated.

CAPE puts your work in the order needed to identify opportunities and deficits to build a workable plan. Of course, you need to be more diverse, but do you get there by recruiting or retaining? Or both? CAPE is a diagnostic process for you to figure out where the problems are in the organization to maximize your resources. Thus, you build a plan to execute against the company's specific challenges or opportunities with measurable outcomes. Once you have that plan based on data you have collected and analyzed, you can execute on it, measure it, and take action. DE&I work is a journey, and like any other walk, you need to start at the beginning.

Usually, a part of any existing diversity plan is mandatory DE&I trainings. It's a quick fix. For years, mandatory training for everyone across the board has been a part of standard DE&I plans. Typically, these are generic workshops that have to be broad enough to address a wide variety of issues related to DE&I. Company employees are generally not thrilled to participate in mandatory, generic training, and, consequently, the trainings don't work.

Plus, if the entire reason to train staff is to effect change to reach specific DE&I goals, generic training won't work if the intended audience is unaware of what their relationship is to the end goal. For example, we know everyone has unconscious bias, but how is one to know their bias if it is unconscious? So, imagine that you do a training on unconscious bias. However, in your audience, one person's bias might be about gender, while the bias of the person sitting next to them could be about race. Both people will be given this kind of generic, across-the-board understanding of unconscious bias. But because bias can be unconscious, they may not know they have it. How would they know which parts of the trainings relate to them? Therefore, no one has any reason to change their behavior.

It's never a good idea to build a program looking for a problem. Identify the problem through data collection and analysis, then build your plan accordingly. Follow the scope and sequence of the CAPE process.

Getting Started on Your Plan

At this point, you've collected the data, you've analyzed it, and because of how the data are structured, you know if there is a recruitment issue or a retention issue. Again, 90% of what a DE&I program does is going to be in one of those two areas. The other 10% of your work is what I call community/thought leadership. This would include things like participating on panels, attending events, professional development, and being a good corporate citizen.

If your data show that recruitment is the needed area of focus, the plan stems from there. It could be that you want a more diverse executive team. But you also need to think about leadership positions. They tend to have very little turnover – maybe 10% or less. But if you've collected the data on leadership turnover in your company as well, you know for certain how likely it is that you will have the opportunity to recruit and hire at the leadership level. This recruitment data all comes from what you've collected from your company. So, you know that planning a DE&I program focused on recruitment fits your needs.

The plan for filling leadership positions is different from how you might fill a diversity need for what might be considered a low visibility/high volume position. Many entry-level positions typically have a lot of hires and low visibility in that there is no major announcement to the entire staff because these level hires are made all the time. However, for high-impact and highly visible positions, like a VP or above, there tends to be a company announcement, and most employees are aware of the new hire. One of the metrics used to measure diversity has always been, "If your company is committed to diversity, you will have a diverse leadership team." This is true, but as I have mentioned, theory and practice are not the same thing.

For highly visible and low-turnover positions like VP, you will need to have a recruitment strategy and activities for when and if the position becomes available. You will need a plan based on building a network of diverse candidates. Maybe start with something like creating a list of companies, organizations, and people to contact even before, not just when, you start looking for a candidate. That's a simple thing you can do now. I recommend a process that outlines, when a senior level or hard to fill position becomes available, there is a plan that will already be put in place to identify candidates.

Doing this is what I call a *hiring protocol*. You should always have some kind of hiring protocol to use as a part of your plan. This is a simple plan that you can put in place, develop, and implement to increase diversity at more senior levels in the organization. This doesn't guarantee a Person of Color, woman, or person with a disability will be hired; it only ensures that they will be considered. That's what diversity plans and hiring protocols for recruitment are all about. If you put in the process and track the data, you will know if the plan is working; in short, do you have selection bias or no diversity in the hiring pool? The order of operations is important. Collect the data, analyze the data, and develop a plan to address what was found in the data.

Once again, the specificity of the plan is important. It makes no sense to focus on an area where your company has fewer DE&I–related challenges. So that means you've collected the data and analyzed it before deciding where to implement change. Then you might be able to say that historically you've had no People of Color in your leadership team. In that particular instance, it makes sense to put a plan into place that helps correct that discrepancy. In your entry-level jobs, it doesn't make sense to change anything because your data shows that you are already getting diverse candidates. The potential mistake can come from applying a rule to every single hire across the board. Instead, be specific about where the lack of diversity exists and is hurting the company. By targeting your work, you can maximize your time and resources, and increase the ROI on the company's investment in you as a diversity leader.

Typically, you will not have the bandwidth or energy to manage every one of the company's searches. As a result, if you apply hiring protocols too broadly, either nothing gets done, or people become more upset with the DE&I program. But if you can look at your company's specific needs and implement strategies and protocols that are intended to improve the diversity of the candidates in selection pools where historically there has been little diversity, you will be improving your company's commitment to diversity. You should specifically target those positions and departments that require intervention and leave those that don't alone.

4-2-50 Program

The *Harvard Business Review* in 2016 published an article,[1] "If There's Only One Woman in Your Candidate Pool There's Statistically No Chance She'll Be Hired," which stated that when companies interviewed three or four candidates and only one of them was a woman, the odds of hiring that one female candidate was zero. But they also found if you interviewed four candidates, with two of them being women and two men, the odds of you hiring a man or women from the candidates interviewed was 50%, which is what it should be. So, by simply balancing out the gender or ethnic/racial balance of an interview panel, you improve the chance of hiring a diverse candidate. It gives no one any advantage; it simply levels the playing field.

While I was at the USOPC, we developed a protocol partly based on that study. The 4-2-50 is a combination of the NFL's Rooney Rule and the article published in the *Harvard Business Review*. For background, the NFL developed the Rooney Rule into their process to diversify the head coaches. Per the Rooney Rule, when interviewing candidates for a head coach position, the team must include a Person of Color among those interviewed.

The 4-2-50 is a process in which you always interview four final candidates and two of whom are from an underrepresented group. By doing this, the odds of hiring a person from an underrepresented group are about 50%, which is what it should be because 50% of the candidates are from an underrepresented group. It gives no one any advantage: It simply levels the playing field. As I mentioned earlier, we used this process at the UOSPC specify to fill positions at director and above, and we were able to increase the hiring of People of Color and women significantly.

I would recommend that if you choose to use the 4-2-50 rule, it should be done strategically to impact areas that have not been historically diverse in the company or organization. It is not necessary to use this process for every hire across the company because the goal is impact, not process. DE&I programs that are heavy on process and not outcomes lose support.

As an example, years ago I worked at the CU Medical Center that had a process that every hire needed a full search to increase diversity. This sounded great in theory, but it became more about the process and not about outcomes. Therefore, by the time I was hired as director of diversity, they had developed a process for hiring managers to ask for an exception to the hiring rule. All the exceptions to the rule had been done so randomly and so unrelated to outcomes that asking for an exception became about the process, and everyone seemed to forget why it had been implemented. As a result, shortly after I started, when I tried to hold people to the policy, remind them of the intent of the policy, and make it about outcomes, several people became upset with me. At one point, I refused to sign off on an exception to conducting a full search for a position in the school of medicine. The dean of medicine was very upset with me, and he went over my head to get the exception. After this point, we had a new process: I would write on the request for exceptions "as per the dean of medicine" and I would not sign the approvals. It became more about process and not about outcomes or any commitment to diversity.

As I have mentioned, I used the 4-2-50 rule at the USOPC and recommended it to other organizations (see Figure 6.1). I used it in a very targeted manner and, again, used the fundamental principles of CAPE. We collected the data and figured out which positions lacked diversity. The data showed the USOPC had little diversity at the director level and above. After identifying and doing our analysis, we put into effect a targeted 4-2-50 for director and above hires. We executed on it, and by

Figure 6.1 4-2-50 Hiring Plan.

just simply doing that, we basically increased the hiring of women and People of Color by about 70%. It was a simple plan for targeted hires that yielded excellent results. We could also show which hires we used the process for and show it was effective and not more costly.

How to Measure ROI in Your DE&I Program

Every single diversity officer at some point in their career will have to answer questions about the return on investment (ROI) on the DE&I program. Are your methods helping the company's plan for increasing diversity? This is the thing that is always going to come up. Many diversity officers struggle answering this question. Their struggle is partly because of how DE&I programs are positioned (I discuss this in Chapter 16), but there are some tactics you can use. As I have mentioned, DE&I officers do not control every hire, but they are held accountable for the diversity or lack of diversity of those hires. Understanding this has proven to be quite helpful in the last 25+ years I have been working in DE&I programs. In particular, I had to present to the USOPC board, sometimes twice a year, and I could lay out the data to show the diversity of the organization and the opportunities to hire as this information gives context to understand why there appears to be only a slight change or where change did happen.

It's also important to keep in mind that DE&I commitment has a cost, and if you are truly committed, you need to pay that cost.

> **JASON-ISM**
> DE&I officers do not control every hire, but they are held accountable for the lack of diversity of those hires.

Additionally, I have developed the process of starting with collecting the data before launching the program. By doing that, I am able to at least show where things were when I started. You have to create an actionable and measurable plan. If you can't measure results, you can't present the ROI data to the company leaders.

One of the early criticisms of the 4-2-50 program was that it was going to be more expensive because we would need to do more and

longer searches and incur the cost of travel for more in-person interviews. What would be the return on investment of longer searches?
No one wanted longer searches with no outcomes. We tracked the
data but also found that because the process was limited and targeted,
it created no impact on budgets. Typically, national searches are used
for director-level positions and higher, and candidates will be flown in
for interviews. (This is also when you need CEO commitment, with a
specific request so they know what is expected. I will expand on this
later in Chapter 10.)

Using the CAPE process helps you with your ROI because you
will need to know if you should stay on track, change track, or invest
more time.

This is how I would use the CAPE process for the Rooney
Rule. Obviously, the NFL started by collecting the data (diversity
in coaches). The analysis of the data led them to understand Black/
African American coaches are underrepresented. They developed a
plan, the Rooney Rule. The NFL then executed the plan, and now
most importantly, they need to use the CAPE technique again. CAPE
is not a one-time application but an ongoing process for an effective
DE&I program. Now I would recommend that the NFL collect and
analyze the data on the Rooney Rule and develop a plan to achieve
the change they would like to see. The current version of the Rooney
Rule has become too much about process and not about outcomes. It
has also been controversial and had mixed results. Why do we know
this? Because of the data.

The How: CAPE DE&I Plan Template

The plan component of CAPE is important because to measure the
effectiveness of a DE&I program, you need to know when the plan
actually started and then track the details. A good DE&I plan needs to
be connected to a data point in time and a metric, such as the number
of People of Color in the sales department, that allows you to combine those two things and execute on them. By collecting the data
first, you will have examples of effectiveness to track, such as we were
10% diverse on October 1 last year and on October 1 of this year, the
company was 15% diverse. That will help you calculate the ROI or

Figure 6.2 Sample CAPE Diversity Template.
Source: Reproduced with permission of CAPE Inclusion, Inc.

effectiveness. As the diversity officer, you can pinpoint exactly what programs you instituted to get that result.

I developed a CAPE plan template, in Figure 6.2, to help you put all the components of CAPE into a simple dashboard. It tracks when you started the plan, what specific steps you decided to take, how you executed, and what kind of results you got.

How to Complete the CAPE DE&I Template

To complete the CAPE Diversity Template, follow these five steps:

1. Start by choosing one of the three major categories of DE&I work (you can add more categories if needed):
   a. Recruitment
   b. Retention
   c. Community/thought leadership
2. Based on your data collection and analysis indicate the program or initiative needed, the department you will focus on, and the person(s) who will be responsible for executing that initiative.
3. Indicate the area of focus for the program and the level of the organization that will be impacted, and the target audience.

Recruitment Diversity Goals:						
Action Plan 2021	Program or Action and Individual Responsible	Area of Focus	Target Demographic	Start & Check In Date		
DE&I Goal #1	Name of Program: Sales Department Diversity Person(s) Responsible: Sue Lee	❏ Board of Directors X Professional Staff ❏ Part-time / Interns ❏ Community ❏ Network ❏ Customer ❏ Vendor ❏ Other	X Race/Ethnicity ❏ Women ❏ LGBTQ ❏ Military Vet. ❏ People with Disabilities ❏ Other	Start Date: 1/1/2021 Check In Date: 1/1/2022	Brief Description of your Program (100 Words or Less)	Identify candidates from underrepresented groups for professional staff positions in the sales department
					How Success is Measured (100 Words or Less)	Accomplish 100% of the program objectives
Outcomes: We had 5 hires and hired 2 employees of Color (report of 10/1/2021)						
Tactics: ❏ Post jobs in 3 diversity focused job boards ❏ Implement CAPE Inclusion 4-2-50 ❏ Identify 4 universities and connect with diversity officer to recruit candidates of Color				Actuals: ❏ Jobs posted in 4 diversity focused job boards ❏ CAPE Inclusion 4-2-50 implemented for all professional staff positions for sales department openings as of 2/1/2021 ❏ Identified and connected with 6 universities and their diversity officers for recruitment of candidates of Color		

CAPE Inclusion   Bridging the Gap Between Commitment and Impact

Figure 6.3 Sample Recruitment Diversity Plan Template.

Source: Reproduced with permission of CAPE Inclusion, Inc.

4. Determine your start date.
5. In 100 words or less, describe the program, the metric, and how success will be measured.

Leave the outcome section blank until the program or initiative end date is reached. Then, collect the data and describe the outcome(s) of your work.

To help you visualize the plan development, a sample completed DE&I recruitment plan appears in Figure 6.3. It addresses the goal of identifying candidates from historically underrepresented groups. The initiative is for the sales department and specifically identifies the recruitment of racial and ethnic minorities. In the description, there are measurable goals and a set timeline. The outcomes section was filled out with the data from the completion date.

The process is the same for retention. Figure 6.4 shows you a sample retention plan. To begin, you have to know what retention looked like the day you started, and that, too, is trackable in the template with the CAPE technique. Therefore, a year from now, if the retention looks the same, you could say that what you did was not working. Or, if it increased, you can say it worked. As I mentioned, the majority of DE&I work is either recruitment or retention. So, on the retention side, if the analysis of the company data showed that a department has

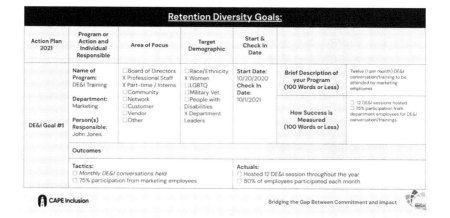

Figure 6.4 Sample Retention Diversity Template.
Source: Reproduced with permission of CAPE Inclusion, Inc.

high turnover, you'll need to develop initiatives to reduce turnover. Figure 6.4 is an example of a retention (inclusion) initiative you might create. If you are concerned about inclusion, it is one of the hardest things to measure, and the sample plan in Figure 6.4 offers you a way to think about how to address it using the CAPE process.

In this scenario, the question becomes what training might you give the manager and the team members specifically in the department that is experiencing a high turnover of women? Again, because DE&I programs have limited resources, the CAPE technique will make the work you do become much more focused. You can have targeted training and conversations tailored to the problem the department or persons experiencing it, rather than offering a company-wide, mandatory, and expensive DE&I training for everyone.

Based on your data, the retention and inclusion conversation becomes very strategic. For example, you can work with the vice president of marketing, discuss the problem, recommend solutions, and collaboratively determine the metrics to measure outcomes.

Now, instead of a confrontation, you've invited a conversation and led the department manager down a road to discovery. Maybe it's the management style causing the problem. For example, the department is micro-managed, which makes people feel as though the manager believes they are incompetent. So, they leave. Maybe it's micro-aggressions causing the problem. As another example, an authoritarian style of leadership could make employees feel as though their voice is being silenced. These could all be things that you could look at, but now, because you've collected the data and analyzed it, you can develop a plan that makes sense. You can make it so that a particular leader knows what is expected of them and how it will improve the department culture. This is why you build the plan after you collect the data and after you analyze it. Then, as you present that data to the manager, it helps create a collegial, goal-oriented partnership to improve outcomes. There's a path forward that leads to progress toward the company's inclusion goals.

These sample CAPE diversity templates also give you a quick dashboard to show why you chose the goal and the plan of action with outcomes. Therefore, the leadership team understands the DE&I initiatives you are focused on, and this will help keep you on track. Additionally, everyone will know what is expected of them. This will help keep you from feeling overwhelmed because the CAPE DE&I plan template is a tool in a format that helps keep the DE&I work manageable. You've analyzed your data, prioritized your goals, and maximized your resources. So now your plan is both strategic and systematic, and you're heading toward getting the outcomes you and your company want.

KEY POINTS

- A diversity plan should be based on data you have collected and analyzed. Otherwise, you may develop a solution without understanding the problem, and you may not be able to measure performance.
- Use the data to determine if you have a recruitment or retention problem and develop a plan accordingly.
- Understand how to use high-impact hires to increase effectiveness of your DE&I program.
- The 4-2-50 is a process in which you always interview four final candidates, two of whom are from an underrepresented group.

Note

1. Stephanie K. Johnson, David R. Heckman, and Elsa T. Chan, in writing for the *Harvard Business Review* on April 26, 2016, entitled their article "If there's only one woman in your candidate pool, there's statistically no chance she'll be hired. When race and gender are blinded, women and non-white (their terms) candidates have a better chance." Accessed on April 7, 2021 at https://hbr.org/2016/04/if-theres-only-one-woman-in-your-candidate-pool-theres-statistically-no-chance-shell-be-hired

Chapter 7

Execute on the Plan

Audio Must Match Video

Recently, I purchased a new TV. I decided there was no reason to read the directions. I figured I love technology, and I'm reasonably handy, so there was no need for directions. What could go wrong?

I soon realized that every channel was in a foreign language. My first thought was that the cable company inadvertently sold me a lineup of channels for this particular foreign language. I assumed all I needed to do would be to change the channel to a local station. I was wrong! The local channel was also in a foreign language. The characters from a very popular US sitcom were speaking in English, I could tell, but the audio was something else. The audio did not match the video. The sound and the action didn't match.

A simple principle of watching TV is that the audio has to match the video. What we say must match what we do. If your company is committed to DE&I, what you say must match what you do. It is important that the DE&I commitment should be reflected in your code of conduct and incorporated into your mission statement. You should publicly state that you are committed to Diversity, Equity,

& Inclusion, and that commitment must also be reflected in your policies and in what your company does. It is one thing to say you are committed to fair pay for everyone, but is that in a policy or a process where pay analysis is done annually? Additionally, employees need to know the company has to, and can, act on its statements. It's simple – make the audio match the video.

E Is for Execute

You have worked through the C-A-P parts of the CAPE process. You have collected data, analyzed it, and planned with it. Now you're at E. We need to execute. Executing can be much easier once you have invested in the CAPE process. The goal now is to begin executing your plans. What's timely here is that you need to start deciding how to put the plan into action – and how to shape the execution of the plan so that it is likely to achieve the goals you defined. Here is where some basic considerations about the execute part of CAPE can help, and then you can figure out whether or not it's working.

Before you begin execution, it's important to keep a few foundational concepts in mind:

- Match the audio and video.
- Know what you control.
- Develop objectives that are targeted and timely, not theoretical.
- Use the data from your collection, and analyze steps to support the execution of your plan.

The hardest thing diversity officers are challenged with is that they don't actually control all the pieces when it comes to execution. This is a major obstacle for goal setting and execution, and an important concept to understand. For example, when it comes to hiring, as a diversity officer, all you can do is tell people that diversity is a priority. In the end, when that decision to hire is made, you don't control it. You have to understand what you can and cannot control. You're not making hiring decisions. You only control some of the context in which those decisions are made. You can provide training and offer data-rich reports. This is one of the reasons a 4-2-50 program can be very effective. The data is going to give you a leverage point.

Identifying patterns, as discussed in the Chapter 5, will help you to execute. If you have data to show a particular leader has never hired a person with disabilities, then it will be hard for them to deny. It will not matter if the hiring pattern is intentional or unintentional. It is just a fact.

When it comes to the DE&I plan objectives, they need to be measurable, practical, and targeted. A lot of times, diversity officers get themselves in trouble by choosing objectives that are so broad or so theoretical that there's nothing to measure. For example, I often see goals like *getting CEO buy-in* or *CEO commitment* as an objective, but what does that mean? It should list the behaviors that you need the CEO to do and when you will need them.

Let's reconsider the previous example of a leader that has never hired a person with a disability. You ask the CEO to have monthly meetings with leaders to review their hiring metrics by diversity categories. The chief diversity officer cannot control the hire, but by creating this type of plan, you have established the expectation of the CEO for every leader. The CEO knows what is expected and when it needs to be done. CEO commitment is now measurable, timely, targeted, and not at all theoretical. This initiative is measurable in that you can see if hiring has been impacted. It is timely because it has a start date, an end date, and a monthly check-in. It is targeted in that it is a specific department, and it can be focused on a specific demographic. It is not theoretical because everyone knows what is expected of them and the associated outcomes.

Execution is the piece that most people get intuitively, but typically DE&I programs fail because the goals are not measurable, timely, targeted, and are overly theoretical. It is easy to say that you want your company to be more diverse; how you get there is the difficulty. If you don't have an idea of the behaviors and actions that are needed to make it happen, the DE&I program will fail.

Execution can be the easiest part when you're using the CAPE process – if you put time and effort where it's most needed. You need to match audio with video. CAPE basically builds a foundation so that when you begin executing, everyone can be aligned on why you're choosing to execute on this particular objective or why you're doing this specific training. I am not a supporter of mandatory DE&I training, but if you choose to use a mandatory training approach, you will have the data and rationale so that it makes sense to everyone. People will show up even if they don't like it because you can clearly support your choice. For example, you can talk about how high turnover is a reality for People of Color throughout the company. You can explain that's why you need a mandatory training to reduce high turnover so that everyone understands and can support new policies or changes. All of this is based on company- and department-specific data that has been analyzed. You've used that data to form a plan. Now you're going to execute.

> **JASON-ISM**
> Diversity programs have competing interests. You can't become diverse if you don't have turnover, and no one wants high turnover.

The How: A CAPE Path to Execute

Use the CAPE process to set reasonable and actionable objectives to make your path to diversity easier to execute. Identify what works and needs to be changed or improved, and then execute again. The goal of these CAPE plans is to make this as easy as possible so you can focus on plan execution and not spend too much time trying to figure out how to write the plan.

A CAPE 30-Day Template

The first 30 days of the CAPE process should be focused on data collection, and you can use the template in Figure 7.1 to help you get organized and stay focused. I've also outlined two specific tasks for day one in your DE&I role. They are:

1. Define the terms *diversity*, *equity*, and *inclusion*. This will ensure everyone has the same understanding of these core concepts. (You'll remember from Chapter 2 that we covered the importance of using a shared language for key DE&I terms in your organization.)

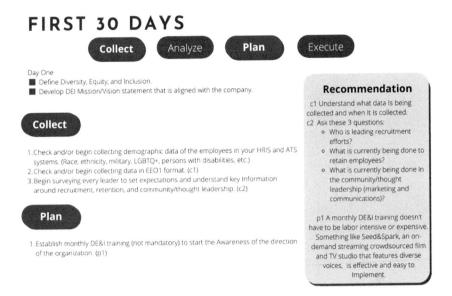

FIRST 30 DAYS

Collect · Analyze · **Plan** · Execute

Day One
- Define Diversity, Equity, and Inclusion.
- Develop DEI Mission/Vision statement that is aligned with the company.

Collect

1. Check and/or begin collecting demographic data of the employees in your HRIS and ATS systems. (Race, ethnicity, military, LGBTQ+, persons with disabilities, etc.)
2. Check and/or begin collecting data in EEO1 format. (c1)
3. Begin surveying every leader to set expectations and understand key information around recruitment, retention, and community/thought leadership. (c2)

Plan

1. Establish monthly DE&I training (not mandatory) to start the Awareness of the direction of the organization. (p1)

Recommendation

c1 Understand what data is being collected and when it is collected.
c2 Ask these 3 questions:
- Who is leading recruitment efforts?
- What is currently being done to retain employees?
- What is currently being done in the community/thought leadership (marketing and communications)?

p1 A monthly DE&I training doesn't have to be labor intensive or expensive. Something like Seed&Spark, an on-demand streaming crowdsourced film and TV studio that features diverse voices, is effective and easy to implement.

Figure 7.1 CAPE 30-Day Template.

2. Develop a DE&I mission or vision statement that aligns with the company. This is important because DE&I efforts need to support the company's business objectives; otherwise, they will fail. Every organization and industry is different, so it's important that you tailor your DE&I work to best fit with your specific company.

Once those are established, you can spend the first 30 days collecting data that will help you understand the organization's culture, challenges, and bright spots. (For more on what data to collect and how, revisit Chapter 4.) It's also important to use the first 30 days to plan basic DE&I training and increase awareness of your efforts. The training will help you communicate your shared language and enlighten people about the general goals of DE&I efforts. It can be as simple as streaming something once a month from Seed&Spark, an on-demand, crowdsourced platform that features diverse voices. Don't get carried away and offer expensive or labor-intensive programs in the first 30 days. After all, you've just begun collecting data, and you won't know what your organization needs until you've had time to analyze it.

This is also a great time to build relationships, which make it easier to collect the data you need and get answers to three important questions:

1. Who is leading recruitment efforts (e.g., of employees and/or customers)?
2. What is currently being done to retain employees and/or customers?
3. What is currently being done in the community and thought leadership (e.g., marketing and communications)?

Questions 1 and 2 are about the two fundamental components of DE&I, recruitment and retention. These can be considered the *video* of existing DE&I efforts. Question 3 will give you insight into the company's messaging, which is the *audio*. Looking at how the answers to Questions 1 and 2 align with that of Question 3 can help you determine if the audio is matching the video, so to speak.

A CAPE 60-Day Template

Once the first 30 days are over, you should have collected enough data that you can begin the second step in the CAPE process: analyzing it (Figure 7.2). Analyze the data you have collected by asking the following questions:

a. Where does your company have diversity? Analyze by department, at director level, and above, and in terms of the leadership team.
b. What is being done to recruit staff and/or customers?
c. What is being done to retain staff and/or customers?

Knowing the answers to these questions should show you whether you have a recruitment or retention issue. You will also be able to see which departments or levels of the organization to focus on. This analysis helps you begin the third step in the CAPE process: planning. Unlike in the 30-day template, the 60-day template's plan should be driven by the data. For example, if the data show that the production department has a retention problem and the director-level positions suffer from promotion bias, you will plan how to address those two specific issues. In this example, you might decide that a diversity officer should be involved in hiring and promotion decisions at the director

Figure 7.2 CAPE 60-Day Template.

level. Additionally, a monthly DE&I training for the production department could address the specific issues (e.g., unconscious bias, poor management, etc.) driving that department's retention problem.

Data collection also continues in the first 60 days. The analysis from the CAPE 60-day template will also help you see where to focus on additional data collection. For example, you will need to consider the organization's characteristics and relevant industry trends in diversity to determine how long it could take for your plan to reach its goals. This will position you to succeed in the first 90 days.

A CAPE 90-Day Template

Once you've made it through the first 60 days of the CAPE process, everything starts to come together. As you can see from Figure 7.3, the CAPE 90-day template includes work on all four steps: collect, analyze, plan, and execute. By this point, it should be clear exactly what you need to execute. You'll put your plan into motion and measure its impact. To continue with our example, this would include starting the actual diversity trainings and retention efforts with the production department. It will also include diversity training and chief diversity officer (CDO) involvement in promotion and hiring decisions at the director level.

Figure 7.3 CAPE 90-Day Template.

Continue to collect data, letting your analysis, plan, and execution guide you. That will tell you what data you need. This could include data about employee turnover, hiring decisions, and promotional decisions. You can incorporate your findings into your departmental specific monthly trainings so your rationale makes sense to everyone.

At the same time, you should also continue to network and build relationships throughout the organization. Now that you have begun to execute, you can also collect data that can show you how your plan execution is working. Asking the following questions can help:

a. Where does the company have diversity (e.g., what departments, what career/job levels)?
b. What is being done to recruit staff and/or customers?
c. What is being done to retain staff and/or customers?

Compare these answers to the same questions from the CAPE 60-day template to measure your progress. You can also use this analysis to adjust your plan. By this time, you should have enough data that you can start planning at a deeper level. For example, you can plan specific efforts to increase recruitment in the departments that need it, you can develop a plan to increase retention where necessary, and you can consider using a targeted 4-2-50 plan to address any glass ceilings. After planning, you can begin to execute these new initiatives and continue the process.

KEY POINTS

- You should publicly state that you are committed to DE&I, and that commitment must also be reflected in your policies and in what your company does.
- You have to understand what you can and cannot control. For example, you control some of the context in which decisions are made but not the hiring decision.
- DE&I plan objectives need to be measurable, practical, and targeted.
- Plans and their execution should be based on company- and department-specific data that has been analyzed. Even if people don't like the plan, they will respect it if you can clearly support your position with data.

Part II

Practical
Lessons Learned
in DE&I Programs

It's not the load that breaks you down, it's the way you carry it.

—Lena Horne

Chapter 8

DE&I Programs Should Look Like the Company

Looking for Four-Leaf Clovers

I like listening to NPR for the stories about average people. The other day, the story was about a woman who seemed to have a knack for finding four-leaf clovers. The woman was very pleasant and unassuming. I would probably have forgotten all about this story except, toward the end of the interview, she said the most amazing thing. She said, "They say four leaf clovers are hard to find, but I have noticed that most people are not looking for four-leaf clovers." This seemed quite simple but very profound.

People often tell me they enjoy my simple stories, but I feel as though I am merely retelling things I have seen. Some even go as far as to tell me I have a gift, which always makes me smile. I am always flattered, but I know simply retelling the experiences is not the gift. The real gift is my family and friends. They have filled my life with happiness, great experiences, and laughs. All I do is try to make sure I am paying attention, and I just simply write down what I have seen. I guess I just happened to be looking for four-leaf clovers.

I hope my stories make people happy and sometimes even shed a tear. Most importantly, I hope to help people see the many four-leaf covers in their lives. Whether it be a funny story about your son, your daughter's smile, or your spouse's warm hand, it is the simple pleasure of living life. We should all spend more time enjoying the gift of a four-leaf clover. They're actually not all that hard to find if you are looking. In life you typically find what you are looking for, whether it be a four-leaf clover, friends, or happiness.

At the end of the day, building a DE&I program is like looking for four-leaf clovers in your company. You have to take the time to understand the culture and the pace of change, and to use the learnings to build a DE&I program that reflects those values. Often, I have found companies and people take the view that DE&I programs are necessary because someone has done something wrong. That's not the case. In reality, DE&I programs are additive. DE&I programs help companies reflect the diversity found in the world, accept the reality that there are inequalities that we can collectively overcome to create a world that is fully inclusive for everyone.

This chapter is about looking for clues that reflect the culture of the organization so you can build a DE&I program that looks like the organization. This will increase your success. I often tell people: "DE&I programs should look like your company to be successful." I have seen diversity, equity, and inclusion programs struggle because they don't look like the company. To look like the company means the initiatives and programs reflect the values and culture of the company. In this chapter, I will further explain this with four examples from the different companies in which I developed DE&I programs from scratch. They are in the sports, healthcare, tech, and education industries. I will share the clues that reflect the culture and how I used them as the basis for the DE&I program. Then I share a mission alignment exercise to help you get started in your company.

JASON-ISM
Your diversity program should look like your company.

Sports – US Olympic and Paralympic Committee

The clue: All about competition.

When I was hired to develop the DE&I program for the US Olympic and Paralympic Committee (USOPC), it became clear very quickly that it is a complicated organization. It has a lot of independent parts with lots of leaders and constituents to keep happy.

The USOPC is a very unique organization, as it is the only nonprofit Olympic Committee in the world. It is also made up of approximately 54 National Governing Bodies (NGB) responsible for overseeing the development of the Olympic and Paralympic sports in the United States. This includes organizations like USA Basketball, USA Track and Field, USA Bobsled, and so on. My job responsibilities included not only the USOPC who directly employed me, but I was also tasked with influencing DE&I results for all of the 54+ national governing bodies (NGBs). This was unique in that the NGBs are independent nonprofits with their own employees and separate boards. When I did some of the more traditional types of diversity work, such as DE&I training, people said all the right things, but we didn't seem to get any movement.

When I built a scorecard, which measured each NGB's diversity and gave them a score to compare with other NGBs, I was able to get a lot more traction. The scorecard allowed me to compare them to one another and to give them a score. Generally, people who work in sports like to compete, so a scorecard pushed the right button. It connected with them as people and aligned with the company culture. People who work in sports intuitively understand competition. I found that for NGBs, if their scorecard was lower than their competitor's scorecard, they wanted to know why, and they wanted to compete. The cards were also shared publicly, so NGB leaders felt public pressure, but that too is part of competing. So, I had to build a program that looked like the culture of the organization. In sports, competition is very much a part of the organization, and those who choose to work there tend to be very competitive. A DE&I scorecard was the perfect way to merge DE&I and the larger mission of the organization. "Scoring" and "winning" is something employees and every ERG could connect to and align themselves to the larger DE&I goals.

The culture of the USOPC was so competitive that even a steps challenge was over the top. I remember the HR team launched a wellness campaign, and part of it included a 10,000-steps-a-week challenge. Total steps and updates for individuals were shared weekly. It became very competitive, and there were people at USOPC logging 170,000 to 200,000+ steps a week!

The DE&I scorecard was the perfect tool for the culture of the USOPC. It was a measurement of each NGB's overall performance against a standardized set of DE&I metrics. It provided a standard score for each NGB individually so they could be compared to each other. The brilliance of the scorecard was that it allowed for the uniqueness of each NGB. Therefore, a small NGB like USA Badminton could be compared to USA Basketball in a manner that was just and incorporated the uniqueness of each NGB. People who are competitive want to compete, but they have to feel the rules are fair. By respecting the need for fairness and allowing a way for them to win, I had to merge the culture with DE&I.

Healthcare

The clue: All about rules, procedures, and processes.

In 2007, I was hired to launch a DE&I program for INTEGRIS Health, a large healthcare system with over 10,000 employees. My experience in healthcare is that it is very rule- and process-oriented and rightly so because that mentality saves lives. What was interesting is that when I interviewed with INTERGIS health, they were very interested about my opinion on affirmative action. My hire was actually contingent on my being able to create a DE&I program without an affirmative action program. I was confident this was something I could easily do.

The reason the organization was adamant that I create a DE&I program without an affirmative action program was because they had a previous negative experience where they had become an affirmative action–compliant organization without realizing it. Several years prior to hiring me, the company had signed an agreement to provide services to a federal prison. Apparently, this was done by a regional person, and some of the details of the agreement were missed. What INTEGRIS Health found out was that whenever you sign an agreement with the federal government, and some state and city governments, your organization becomes an affirmative action employer.

As the story was explained to me, the hospital system received a letter requesting an affirmative action plan and telling them they were going to be audited. The first response of the hospital system was, "We are not an affirmative action employer." The federal government provided them with the signed agreement, and INTEGRIS Health had to develop an affirmative action plan in about 30 days. My understanding is that this became a three- or four-year ordeal and was quite a problem for the hospital leaders, to say the least.

In about my second year of developing the DE&I program, it became clear that some of the smaller hospitals could make more money if they provided services to military veterans. However, the fact that the health system was not an affirmative action employer meant they could not take federal dollars from the Veterans Administration. The leaders of the hospital system came to the realization they were leaving a lot of money on the table. They then reversed their decision and said, "Hey, Jason, we need you to convert the organization to an affirmative action employer." So I began to develop the program. This actually did not require a major shift in direction. Most of what people know about affirmative action is untrue. It does not require that you hire some quota, nor does it penalize you for not doing so. The company will never be in a position to tell white applicants that they cannot hire them because the company has to hire a certain number of "unqualified" minorities. Those are all myths.

The major changes are things most companies should do anyway and will prove to be quite good for the morale of all employees. For example, all job openings have to be advertised. This seems simple, but many companies do not advertise all openings. This typically is terrible for morale because employees often state, "I would have applied for that opportunity if I had known the company was hiring for that job." I hear this all the time, and it makes employees feel there is preferential treatment for some but not for others. Not advertising openings undermines morale and DE&I programs. This simple change makes all employees feel respected and included.

The other thing affirmative action employers are required to do is track the race, ethnicity, gender, ability status, and military veteran status of all applicants and employees. This data is also used to evaluate terminations, promotions, and retention for *adverse impact*, which is another way of saying *bias*. Again, this is something you should be doing anyway. The CAPE process can help you use this data and establish a DE&I program with outcomes. Generally, staff, leaders, and the board will welcome this type of approach.

As I implemented the necessary changes for affirmative action compliance, other DE&I–related initiatives also grew. Why? Because having data helps leaders understand what is required and where the opportunities are to increase diversity.

An affirmative action program forces an organization to follow certain rules, processes, and policies. What do healthcare organizations do well? They follow rules, processes, and policies. It is part of the culture because, in the worst-case scenario, what happens if you don't follow protocol in a healthcare setting? People die. Therefore, everyone understands and accepts that it is part of the culture to follow processes and procedures. They need process and procedures to improve their practices throughout the company, and that gave me incredible leverage.

Although in general, I am not a supporter of mandatory DE&I trainings, in this healthcare setting they were effective. Why? Because it is part of the culture to attend regularly scheduled mandatory trainings. If you are a nurse, there are certain training requirements you have to meet. They are non-negotiable. Everybody has agreed to them as part of the culture. So mandatory DE&I training fit the culture and became part of an effective DE&I program for the healthcare system.

As I will explain in the next section, this would not have been a good strategy for a tech startup. Had I taken what I did in healthcare and imposed it on the tech company, I would have failed. That is why it is so important to understand the organization and implement programs that look like the organization.

Tech – Techstars

The clue: All about speed.

When I was hired to lead and create a DE&I program for Techstars, the organization was all about startups; they did not like rules. Unlike the USOPC, they were not really motivated by competition either. They were about speed and believed they made decisions fast and moved fast. They prided themselves on working faster. In fact, everyone that worked at Techstars was given the book, *Do More Faster*, written by David Cohen, co-founder of Techstars, and Brad Feld, author, blogger, and leading early-stage venture capitalist at Foundry Group.

Techstars is an accelerator and was founded to provide start-ups (entrepreneurs) with the financial, human, and intellectual resources to prosper. Techstars, like a lot of other organizations in the tech industry, was trying to do more in the DE&I space. This was prior to George Floyd and the social justice protests of 2020, but even at that time, it was no secret that the startup space, tech companies, and venture capitalists (VC) were not diverse. To make it even worse, there were lots of articles and research that showed that almost no VC funds were going to women or People of Color. The problem was not that women and People of Color were not starting companies. In fact, they were starting companies at the same rate if not higher. But there was data to show women and People of Color did not get any start-up investments. Techstars was perfectly situated to address this from the investment side, but it needed a simple way to launch the DE&I program.

I was hired by Techstars to launch the DE&I program from scratch with few resources and no staff. This is typical for how most companies commit to starting DE&I, so I was prepared because I had done this before. By using the simple principle of creating a DE&I program that looks like the company, I created *Techstars Includes*. I did not use the terms *diversity, equity,* and *inclusion,* because that took up too much space on the page. It was too long, and it did not reflect a culture of speed. So with just one word, *includes,* I launched the program.

I knew by only using *includes,* the word would reflect the speed at which the company liked to work. I liked *Techstars Includes* because on day one of employment, employees could quickly connect to, and understand that, ultimately, the goal was to make sure everyone felt included. But this approach would not work in an educational setting where getting the ideas well-defined, and taking the time to do it, matters more than speed.

Education – University of Wyoming, University of Colorado Health Sciences Center, Western Governors University

The clue: Everything in academia has to be academic.

I started my career at a university, and later in my career I was hired by a large academic institution to launch their DE&I program. From those experiences, I can tell you that DE&I programs in educational settings have to be academic. This is one setting in which the theory and history will get as much attention as the actual work. For an educational institution, the words, theory, and work of DE&I are equally important.

Early in my career, I vividly remember leading a DE&I committee in which the committee members insisted on starting with creating definitions for a lengthy list of DE&I–related words. The committee actually spent three months working to define *cultural competency*. In the end they never actually agreed on a definition of *cultural competency*, but I needed to align myself to their pace, their needs, and their vision for the work. Their intent was well-founded, but to have the impact I'd been hired to achieve, I had to acknowledge that it was important to them, as academics, to discuss meanings and to have a common language related to diversity. I listened, I learned, and I used this as a clue to launch the DE&I program. The committee members were passionate, and they were highly engaged.

One thing I often hear is that a challenge to a diversity officer is you're always preaching to the choir. I always tell people, "The choir needs the preaching too." I used this saying to remind myself to be patient with this committee as there's nothing wrong with leveraging the support of those who are already supportive of DE&I. The fact of the matter is, the goal is to grow the choir and not make the people who are in the room feel devalued. Typically, things start slow. You have to continue to support those people and hope to try to expand and grow your diversity. It is a challenge, but it is one you have to just accept because it comes with the territory.

Eventually, I had to tell the committee we needed to move forward with the actual work of setting goals and creating the activities that would have an impact. I was ultimately able to be successful in higher education by designing a DE&I program that resonated with the committee members' academic need for definitional clarity.

Organizational Mission Alignment

Mission alignment will be more important in the future for companies. Due to all of the social activism of 2020, many companies made statements about their commitment to diversity, equity, and inclusion. Those statements will not be enough. Companies will need to bridge the gap between what they say and what they do, and companies will also have to prove they did it. They will need to have outcomes that are proof they executed on their statements for internal and external constituents. The way to get there is by aligning your mission and vision with your DE&I goals. If your DE&I plan looks like your company, you will get there.

As I have shown in the previous examples, when I say your diversity program should look like the organization, it should reflect its culture, and you should be able to see how the company mission and vision overlap with the DE&I program mission and vision. You should be able to identify the behaviors that are proof of the commitment to DE&I. One of the exercises I would encourage you to do is the DE&I mission alignment activity. How does the mission of the organization align with its diversity, equity, and inclusion goals? When you start a diversity program, the way you can get buy-in is to align the DE&I work and create a vision statement that reflects the mission statement of the organization.

As a DE&I officer, you can take the public statements, align them with the mission and vision of the company, and create DE&I programming that will have real impact (and will satisfy the CEO and board members as well). Having diversity, equity, and inclusion woven into your company's intentions and goals bridges intent and impact, plus it gives you a bridge to understand how to connect with employees and the company. Most importantly, it will hold the company accountable for their public commitments.

If you recall the first two phases of the CAPE process, collect and analyze, the concept of measuring for diversity and its impact is something you will do, based on your alignment with mission and vision. You will establish and measure your outcomes. To illustrate what I mean, there is a story someone shared with me about a university president. As the story goes, the president of a university went to the dean of the school of engineering and asked, "What is the goal of the engineering school?" The dean stated that the goal was to create today's best engineers. The president of the university responded, "If that's what you are doing, you are failing our students. You should not be creating *today's* best engineers; you should be creating *tomorrow's* best engineers. If you create today's best engineer, that engineer is outdated the minute they graduate from our school. Our obligation to our students is preparing them for the future."

If you think about that, our DE&I work is part of that, too. In order to build a dynamic company, you have to understand what may happen in the future (the company vision) and plan for that change. That is where vision alignment with your DE&I outcomes becomes reality. A company's vision is their future state. So, as you build your DE&I program, look to the company mission for the "do nows" and the company vision for the long-term impact, such as the increases in recruitment, retention, and performance.

The reason comes down to these questions: What kind of company are you building? Are you building today's best company or tomorrow's best company? How are you integrating the DE&I work as a bridge of support for the company?

Think about the example I shared about my Techstars experience above. I knew it was important for the *Techstars Includes* program to reflect speed. This is quite a contrast to my work in academia, where things moved slowly so that people could discuss every aspect of definitions and theory. *Techstars Includes* would never have worked in academia, and the program we eventually came up with for academia would never have resonated with Techstars. No matter what type of organization you're working with, employees need to able to connect to the DE&I program and understand what is expected of them. In short, your diversity program should look like your company. Identifying clues early on about an organization's culture will help you do that.

The How: An Organizational Mission-Alignment Exercise

First, review the company's mission and vision statement. Then, define diversity, inclusion, and equity. You should be able to say, as an organization, if this is truly our mission and we believe in diversity, equity, and inclusion, and what are the behaviors we would see that would let us know our diversity work is working? What are the behaviors we should be able to see in our organization that are proof that our mission values align with our diversity, equity, and inclusion?

In Figure 8.1, I've provided a blank template to use in aligning your company's mission and vision with its definitions of DE&I and the behaviors you would expect to see that demonstrate commitment. Clearly writing down specific behaviors is important because it can also serve as a basis for evaluating your plan's progress. Behaviors tend to be measurable. Without measurable behaviors, you won't be able to tell whether the plan you are executing is working, and you won't have clear data to collect.

COMPANY NAME: **YEAR:** **DATE:**

DE&I Worksheet

DE&I MISSION VISION ALIGNMENT EXERCISE

In the box below, add your company's current Mission and Vision. In the bottom box, add how your company defines each of these terms.

Company Mission/vision:

DE&I as Defined by Company:

Based on your Company's Mission/Vision and DEI definitions, list the behaviors you would see if these definitions were lived in your Mission or Vision. This becomes the basis for your DE&I Mission Statement

Behaviors that would reflect Company's belief:

1.

2.

3.

4.

Figure 8.1 CAPE Template for DE&I Mission Values Alignment.

Step-by-Step Guide to Mission/Vision Alignment

1. Begin the form by visiting the organization's website. As you prepare to complete the template, here are the steps you should take.
2. Request a copy (or find on the company website) of the company's overall mission and vision statements and insert those into the first box, "Company mission/vision."
3. Request a copy (or create/develop) the company's definitions of diversity, equity, and inclusion.
4. Using your data collection from the CAPE process, begin to associate your findings with the mission/vision or the definitions. Although the behaviors don't need to align one-by-one with mission/vision or definitions, the chart is constructed so that you can easily associate them and identify gaps.

Mission and vision statements and DEI definitions *should* be easily found and publicly available to attest to the company's commitment. If you can't easily find mission, vision, or DE&I definitions, I would recommend that posting them should be the first thing to put in the column for behaviors.

As an example of a completed alignment template, let's use a company, Gales, Inc. Gales, Inc. is a company that provides better footwear for healthcare providers (Figure 8.2).

As you can see, Gales, Inc. established three specific behaviors that would reflect the company's belief and commitment to DE&I. Some of these, like updating the website to include their DE&I mission and vision, would be easy to accomplish in the short term. Others, such as the employee response to monthly DE&I conversations, may take more time, depending on the company culture. And others, such as the diverse sales materials, may be impacted by other factors. For example, if the next online catalog photo shoot isn't scheduled until the next quarter, it might be difficult to show more diversity before then. No problem. In that case, you can plan to work within the established timeframe.

To reiterate, you must build a diversity program that looks like the organization. This is necessary to get buy-in and also to ensure that everybody understands it. I would encourage you to think about the culture of the organization. Are you building a program that looks like

COMPANY NAME: YEAR: 2021 DATE: JAN 1 2021
GALES INC

DE&I Worksheet

DE&I MISSION VISION ALIGNMENT EXERCISE

In the box below, add your company's current Mission and Vision. In the bottom box, add how your company defines each of these terms.

Company Mission/vision:

To better protect the 59 Million+ Healthcare Professionals who are exposed to infectious fluids and disease in standard footwear.

DE&I as Defined by Company:

- Diversity (Is what we look like.)

  - Diversity – reflecting the mixture of differences and similarities found in the world and acknowledging the related tension as we strive to develop more inclusive and high performing environments.

- Equity (Is how we treat each other.)

  - Equity is creating full access, and removing barres. Equity is the fair treatment, access, opportunity, and advancement for all people, while at the same time striving to identify and eliminate barriers that have prevented the full participation of some groups.

- Inclusion (Is why we stay.)

  - Inclusion is making people feel welcomed and valued.

Based on your Company's Mission/Vision and DEI definitions, list the behaviors you would see if these definitions were lived in your company. This becomes the basis for your DE&I Mission Statement

Behaviors that would reflect Company's belief:

1. Website and policies clearly state our DE&I Mission and Vision and our commitment to DE&I

Figure 8.2 Gales Inc. DE&I Mission-Vision Alignment completed version.

Source: Reproduced with permission from Gales, Inc. and CAPE Inclusion.

2. Our monthly DE&I conversations are widely attended and valued at our company at all levels of the organziation.

3. Our sales materials and online catalogs are diverse.

DE&I Mission Statement:

Everyone deserves access to protective footwear for healthcare professionals regardless of location, situation, race, gender, sexual orientation, ethnicity, or any other identity. We have a commitment to addressing injustice and removing barriers.

Figure 8.2 (Continued)

the organization, or are you building a program that is all drawn from theory in textbooks?

Aligning your DE&I program with the mission and vision of the company and its definition of diversity allows you to construct a program that is most likely to make an impact for the organization. Never take a one-size-fits-all approach with your DE&I program. You want to pose and answer the question: What are the behaviors we would see in our organization that are proof that our mission, vision, and values align with our diversity, equity, and inclusion goals and programs?

KEY POINTS

- Look for clues that reflect the culture of the organization so that you can build a DE&I program that reflects the values and culture of the company.
- Ensure mission/vision alignment by using the DE&I Mission-Vision Alignment Template.
- Define or develop diversity, equity, and inclusion definitions.
- Outline the behaviors we would see in the organization that are proof that your mission, vision, and values align with your diversity, equity, and inclusion goals and programs.

Chapter 9

DE&I Challenges That No One Tells You

Whose Mother Are We Talking About?

I work in the diversity, equity, and inclusion (DE&I) space, so I often get asked: "Are people too sensitive? It seems like you can't say anything anymore without offending someone! Everything is so politically correct."

My response is, "It depends on whose mother we are talking about. If the joke is about my mom, then I am never too sensitive. But if we're talking about your mother, you may be too sensitive."

The response might be something like, "I think you should lighten up. Jokes about your mother are really funny. I don't think people mean anything by making fun of your mother. Come on, we laugh about your mother all the time. I remember back in the good old days we could say whatever we wanted about your mother. What happened? Where's your sense of humor?"

The next time you think someone is being too sensitive, take the joke or comment and turn it around so that it's about your mother, your three-year-old daughter, your six-year-old nephew, or someone else who is special to you. Would you feel bad hearing this said about that person? If so, then maybe you can see their point. Maybe they are not just being too sensitive.

JASON-ISM

Whose mother are we talking about? I agree we have become way too sensitive because the jokes about your mom are really funny.

I like jokes. I like watching stand-up comedians and satire as much as anyone, and I have laughed at racist and homophobic jokes. Sometimes these jokes are funny. Sometimes they're not. So, where's the line? How do we know what we can say?

The answer *always* is – it depends. People are complicated, and there is not going to be a simple answer that works in every situation. But, if someone thinks you crossed a line, there is one thing you can always say: "I am sorry. I didn't intend to offend or hurt you." You can take a moment to understand why someone might find a joke or comment offensive or hurtful. Telling someone they should "lighten up and see the humor" is always the wrong thing to say.

The line between offensive and funny can be hard to find. I work on me. Sometimes I am the one laughing at an off-color joke, and sometimes I am the one whose feelings are hurt by it. Sometimes I am even the one making a bad joke.

More importantly, I try to understand when I offend – and I apologize. And I accept an apology from others when they offend me. It is my sincere hope that as people, we can do these two simple things. Our words have power in how we injure others – and in how we use our words to heal.

JASON-ISMS

People have a right to be sensitive and protective, and to voice when they have been offended. We can all apologize and learn.

It comes back to the question of whose mother we are talking about. That is always the question. Listening to each other is always the answer, and being ready to accept an apology or offer one is a way forward for all of us. At the end of the day, people are complicated, and in many cases there will not be one simple answer for every situation.

This chapter is about the challenges of implementing a diversity program that no one else will tell you about. I have started diversity programs in four different industries, in small and large companies, and I can tell you there are a few things that you should know, especially if you're starting a diversity program from scratch. Starting a DE&I program is complicated, and simple answers, or ones that always work, can be difficult, but I can guide you past some of the pitfalls. For example, I can tell you what really happens with budget and why you should hire quickly. And, as I discussed in Chapter 7, you need to be aware of what you can, and cannot, control to have a successful DE&I program. Also, you need to have an understanding of the ins and outs of board diversity and all forms of discrimination. I'll tell you about these things in this chapter.

Staff and Budget

Being a diversity officer, there are some things I recommend you do that no one else is going to tell you about. This is number one. If you get a chance to hire, do it quickly. Once you start the job, you will be overwhelmed before you know it. Generally, if it is a new program or you are launching one, negotiate for staff as part of the hiring process, so within a few days or a month you can hire somebody. The economy is hard to predict, and what I have seen happen is they tell you that you can hire someone, and then the economy changes, and guess what, they want you to put that hire off. Suddenly, you're the only one working on DE&I for the company. The expectations don't change, but your staffing has, and they want you to execute at the same level with your team of one. If you do not have staff, ask for them because it will become an issue very quickly.

Of the four DE&I programs I have launched, I have twice been asked to postpone hiring due to the economy or other factors. I remember starting at Techstars and being told I would be able to hire someone to help me shortly after I started. I had discussed this during the interview and prior to agreeing to take the position. I waited to hire because I was focused on other things at the time. Unfortunately, at about the 60-day mark, when I wanted to start the hiring process, I was asked to wait until early in the second quarter. When all was said and done, it was almost a year before I was able to get someone on staff. Hire quickly.

The second thing I recommend is to think through how you will execute with little or no budget and set the right expectations with your employer. I can tell you from experience that, just like hiring staff, the budget discussed during the interview may not look like the budget you actually get. I have been told by those interviewing me and those who hired me that I would be able to negotiate the budget and build the program. The economy is unpredictable. I agreed to accept the position as vice president of DE&I at Western Governors University (WGU) in March of 2020, and by my start date in April the world was in a full-on pandemic. That changed everyone's budget. The other nuance is understanding when the budget is set. Companies will sometimes hire you and tell you that you can negotiate for budget during the annual process. If you get hired in August and the budget requests were submitted in July, you will need to wait a year.

Budget is one of the big issues when starting a DE&I program. Some companies that have never had a diversity program don't know how to launch it. They don't know what it takes in terms of time and staff resources. That will put you at a fundamental disadvantage because the leadership team may take the attitude that they do not have much budget to give you, but they often know how much budget is too much. Or, you will be told they do not know how to staff a DE&I program, so the company won't give you any staff.

They are not acting above-board here. Companies already know how to start programs. For instance, if you're a small, growing company and you decide you are going to start a marketing department, you probably assume the department would need staff and a budget to effectively start the program. A DE&I program should be no different, but I've seen it happen several times where they give you a small budget and no staff, even if every other program has three or four people to run it. I experienced this while at Techstars. I started with no budget or staff, but during the first year I was there, they launched two additional initiatives/departments, which both started with staffs of at least four and a significant budget.

So just know that when you are expected to launch a program with no staff and limited budget, the company may be setting you up to fail and does not have a true commitment to diversity. Companies know how to launch programs. They do it all the time. There is no other initiative/department that companies would launch without staff and little to no budget. Even if they don't know exactly how to build a DE&I program, they know that a program would need staff and budget.

Responsibility for Things Beyond Your Control

One thing most DE&I officers don't realize is that they do not have enough decision-making authority and resources to be successful. This goes beyond budget; it is that you are asked to be accountable for decisions you don't control. This will continually be a problem for diversity officers. They hold you accountable for many things that you have no control over. Now, there is a way to deal with this, and that, again, comes back to the CAPE process and why you collect data. Below you will find things you will be held accountable for but do not control that I wish I had been told.

Hiring Decisions

Lack of diversity will always be your fault, even though you don't make the final hiring decisions. To address this, you need to hold leaders accountable by using hiring, retention, promotion, and termination data. If diversity in a particular department is much lower than the company average, even though you don't control that decision, you now have a lever to impact hiring decisions because you can present the data to the hiring manager and company leaders quarterly or annually. (This is what CEO commitment looks like at a practical level.) When you can show that a particular department or manager hires People of Color at a rate much lower than the other hiring managers, the discrepancy will need to be explained. The data point now gives you leverage and identifies the departments/individuals that need to be held accountable for the lack of diversity. That is why the CAPE system works.

Leverage the data by asking the CEO to review the DE&I data with each leader on a consistent basis. The reality is that some departments are going to support the work you are doing while others will not. **The data on hiring, retention, promotion, and terminations is hard to deny, regardless of the level of support, especially if the CEO makes it a priority by reviewing the data quarterly or annually.** This is what CEO support/commitment looks like in very practical terms.

Organizations Change Slowly

Like large ships, organizations change directions slowly. I've been hired as a diversity officer many times, and the people who hire me realized that the culture is broken. They hire you and think, "Oh, the diversity officer is going to fix everything." Well, yeah. I'm going to do that, but I cannot do that in six months. You will find that many employees also think you can fix every problem, and your mere presence is all it takes to correct every form of discrimination they have endured. Be sure to set realistic goals, outcomes, and timelines.

> **JASON-ISM**
> Like I always say, the biggest challenge for DE&I programs is unrealistic expectations.

Senior Leadership and Board Diversity

Just like hiring decisions at lower levels of the company, you will be held accountable for the diversity of the senior leadership team. Companies, employees, and DE&I consultants commonly say, "The leadership team should be more diverse, if you are committed to diversity." Yes, it should, but that doesn't mean it changes quickly. What typically happens is that leaders, employees, and constituents set up an expectation that the leadership team is going to become more diverse in a short period of time. That kind of change only happens if a lot of leaders leave quickly, and generally it is a bad thing to have a lot of leaders leave over a short period of time. So let me assure you, the leadership does not become more diverse quickly, even in low-performing companies. You have to set the right expectation of how quickly the leadership team will be more diverse and how quickly you can impact the culture.

The diversity of the board is often something many people take into account when trying to assess a company's DE&I commitment. As the DE&I leader, this is something many people will ask you about and for which you will be held accountable. Unfortunately, impacting the diversity of a board is another area that is difficult. Board seats don't often become open; thus the opportunity to increase diversity on the board can be limited by the terms of appointments. Additionally, companies like to keep good board members, so setting the right expectation about how quickly the diversity of the board might be changed is important. One thing you can begin doing is developing a list of potential board candidates from underrepresented groups that can be submitted when a board opening does come open. Equally important is setting the right expectation, as boards change slowly. Remember, high turnover on a board, among senior leadership, and at any other level in the company is not considered a good thing.

Code Words

Every company has *code words*. I would recommend you address a company's use of code words in the hiring process. Code words are terms and phrases that reinforce a belief system or biases, whether intentionally or unintentionally. For example, consider the question: "Is this person a *good fit* for our company?" How is *fit* defined? Is it used to justify hiring someone that looks like everyone else in the company or shares their biases rather than their ability to do the job? I also hear "What college did they go to?" or "Were they a member of a sorority or fraternity?" Do you ask who referred this candidate? These questions and code words like *fit* have nothing to do with someone's ability to do the job, but they are a coded way to exclude candidates during the hiring process. Ultimately, this perpetuates bias.

JASON-ISMS
The biggest challenge of DE&I programs when it comes to hiring is the concept of *fit*. *Fit* is a code word used in the hiring process to exclude anyone who looks different or may have a different perspective.

Promotions

Promotions are tough to impact because, again, you don't control when they are going to happen, or how many are going to happen. Even if, as most companies do, the company has an annual process where they do promotions, they could still have some budget constraints. If they let you know that they are only going to be able to make a certain number of promotions because of their budget limitations, or, there are only so many promotions they can make in a year, none of that is under your control. Because of those constraints, you have to help people understand what is possible and the extent of your influence over them. Finally, use the CAPE process and diversity data to hold company leaders and hiring managers accountable. This, again, is a place where the CEO can show their commitment and impact the diversity of the company.

Managing Expectations

You have to help set appropriate expectations, whether you're planning to increase diversity, reduce promotion bias, or improve retention. You also need to clearly remind people how much power you have to effect change in these areas, so that you're not setting yourself up for failure. Typically, I find that what most people want from a diversity, equity, and inclusion program simply cannot be done in the set timetable. For example, something like 50% gender diversity on the leadership team could take years, depending on the rate of turnover among the leadership team. This can prove to be a very difficult position. To be effective, it is important to understand the ways you can influence the hiring process. Understand where you can have an impact and how you can eliminate different forms of discrimination in the hiring process.

KEY POINTS

- If you think someone is being too sensitive, take the joke or comment and turn it around so that it's about your parent or someone special to you. Would you feel bad hearing this said about that person?
- Hire quickly and understand the details and procedures around your department's budget.
- Know what you control and how to set appropriate expectations to measure your success.
- Increasing diversity among staff, senior leadership, and the board takes time and depends on turnover.
- *Fit* is a code word used in the hiring process to exclude anyone who looks different or may have a different perspective.
- Leverage the DE&I data to help your CEO know how and when to show commitment and who to hold accountable.

Chapter 10

When to Get CEO Involvement

What Friends Do

Years ago, I had the privilege of mentoring at the Stanley Hupfeld Academy at Western Village in Oklahoma City. The Hupfeld Academy is an elementary charter school in an economically depressed area of Oklahoma City. The school is sponsored by the Oklahoma City Public School Board and INTEGRIS Health. Most of the children come from single-parent homes, and 90% of the children are on free or reduced-price lunches. INTEGRIS Health adopted this school several years ago and allows all of its employees the opportunity to mentor a child for one hour a week without having to take time off.

On one particular occasion, when I went to visit my mentee, he had gotten into trouble. Apparently, his behavior had been quite bad all week. My mentee was no angel, but this was somewhat unusual. We talked a little bit about it – not too much because he was still in a bad mood and not very talkative. We worked on some homework, and then he wanted to go outside to play basketball. I told him no because his behavior had been bad during the week, and basketball was a reward for good behavior. This clearly made him mad, and he pouted quite a bit, finally refusing to speak to me at all. I found this somewhat disrespectful, and I began to think maybe I should tell him that I was *not* going to keep coming back if he was going to be disrespectful to me. For whatever reason, I did not say that I might not keep coming back if his behavior did not improve. I just kept the thought to myself and walked him back to his class.

The next week when I returned to mentor, my mentee's behavior had been better, but still he was less than happy to see me. He did not want to talk much, but I tried to make conversation anyway. I would ask questions, and he would mumble some answer and not make eye contact. It was getting very frustrating. I again thought maybe I should not come back – maybe he doesn't want me for his mentor. I did not threaten not to come back, but I sure thought about it. It is frustrating to talk to someone who does not seem to like you or want you there.

Going into the third week, I had prepared myself with "the speech." I had decided while driving my car to the Stanley Hupfeld Academy, that if my mentee was going to be quiet and unresponsive, I was going to give him a talking to! I would remind him that I was a volunteer, and I would not be returning unless he was more respectful to me. As I walked to the classroom, I had my speech ready and was fully prepared to give it. I opened the door to the classroom, but it was empty. The teacher was there, and she said, "Your mentee is in art class, but I will give you some homework for you to do with him. You can pick up your mentee from the art class for the mentoring session." As she began getting things together to give me, she said, "Your mentee's father left a couple of weeks ago, and he did not want anyone to know."

When I arrived at the art class to pick up my mentee, he was still in the mode of not talking much and made little eye contact. I told him that the teacher had given me some homework for us to work on. Again, my mentee had no real response. I thought I would cheer him up and said, "Let's skip the homework and go straight to the basketball court!" He seemed a little happier but not much better. As we walked to the basketball court, I walked next to him and said, "I am your friend. Do you know what that means?" He mumbled, "Yes."

I said, "Well, what does it mean?" My mentee became a little upset with me. I guess he figured this question was too simple for a fifth grader. He just frowned and kept walking. I said, "It means I am your friend, and you can get mad at me all you want. You can choose to not talk to me, but I will still keep coming back."

He was right to be mad at the world. When you are a fifth grader and your dad walks out, you should be mad, you should be hurt, and it will not make sense. You would probably assume that your dad is just the first of the things and people that are going to leave you. It was easier for him to push everyone away and not get hurt. He was only trying to protect himself from being hurt, trying to make sense of the world.

I told my mentee every week until school let out that I would be back. I told him it did not matter if he was mad at me or did not want to talk – I would always come back. I would come back every week because that is what friends do.

I find that this is the kind of steady and unrelenting support that DE&I programs need from companies, specifically CEOs and company leaders. Many times, employees don't like change and do not want their values or morals challenged. Like my mentee, they may not want to talk about it and may not make eye contact to avoid facing the challenge you represent. Getting CEO support and involvement will make a difference.

Setting CEO Expectations

When I was interviewed by the CEO of the United States Olympic and Paralympic Committee (USOPC), I asked him, "If I get this job, what would success look like to you in three years?" His answer was troubling. He said, "When I walk out of this office, it will look different. It will be much more diverse." I knew I couldn't do that. Why did I know that? The USOPC only had 10% turnover. When the CEO walks out of his door, the first people he sees are mostly other senior executives. Generally, those people don't leave. If you have 10% turnover for the overall company, the people outside the door of the CEO, the other company leaders probably have even a lower turnover rate. Even the best DE&I programs are not going to make a significant change in the diversity of the executive leadership team in three years. His expectation was unrealistic. I had to help him understand what to expect from a DE&I program. I was at the USOPC for six years, and as I recall, there were only three total executives hired or promoted during that time.

> **JASON-ISM**
> Having 50% diversity on the leadership team sounds great, but you would need approximately 50% of the current leaders to leave to get to that kind of number quickly. That is just unrealistic.

Helping the CEO and the leadership team (and all employees) understand what is achievable is going to be of paramount importance. If you can't help the company understand what can actually be achieved, you're setting up yourself and the company for failure. You have to know the turnover rate and how that impacts your ability to make the company more diverse. That's why I created the CAPE program. You've got to collect the data in order to analyze it. You need to know what the turnover rate is before you can set any type of goal to become more diverse. If you know what the turnover is, you can set the right expectation about the timeline and goals to increase diversity.

When to Involve the CEO

One of the questions I always get is about CEO commitment. It has been said over and over that diversity programs cannot work without CEO commitment. This is generally true, but at the same time this advice is so theoretical, it makes it difficult to execute. What is the CEO supposed to do? What would CEO commitment look like? If the CEO has never led a company with a DE&I program, they may not know what is expected or how and when to get involved.

So, the question actually isn't, "Do you have CEO commitment?" Generally speaking, if you have been hired as a chief diversity officer, in theory, you have CEO commitment as they had to sign off on creating the position. The question is, "When is the best time to use CEO commitment?" and then you need to figure out how to leverage that to execute your programs.

I always tell people whenever you start a DE&I program, don't have the CEO put her name on every initiative or program. I know this goes against what almost every consultant is going to tell you. They want immediate CEO involvement, and they will tell you it is the best way to launch the initiative and get more employees to participate. This is generally true, but the question you need to ask yourself is: "Is this a program the CEO needs to sign off on?"

If the CEO sends out an email to everyone about your new program, it will have a good response. That is true, but you don't want that CEO endorsement until you have worked out the potential problems. Wait until you see how that program works before you put the CEO's name on it because the last thing you want to do is initiate a program that is clumsy or that has some parts that aren't working. You don't want the CEO's eyes on your events or initiatives until they are well executed. That takes time and trials.

It might surprise you when I say: Do not get CEO involvement when you first launch a program. Here is why: When you do initiatives and programs within a diversity program, there are going to be tons of vendors who approach you with great ideas. And every one of them is going to tell you, "When you launch my initiative or you buy into our program, we help you launch it and make a big announcement to all the employees from the CEO." That is mistake number one. Unless you know how the initiative is going to work, pilot it first.

Pilot every initiative you launch in your DE&I plan. The last thing that you want is to launch a half-baked program. I've seen this happen to a lot of organizations and DE&I leaders. They launch this new initiative for all employees to participate in, and it is not yet ready for prime time.

For example, while I worked at Techstars, I had a lot of DE&I consultants and vendors email and call me with programs and trainings. There was a vendor in particular that I did a pilot with, and they insisted that I needed CEO commitment. They told me I would get better participation if I had the CEO give an endorsement of the program and send an email to every employee directly from the CEO. Although they had no experience as a DE&I officer, they assured me that clients who had launched with a CEO email had better response. They repeatedly told me, "Jason, if you just get an email from the CEO and send it to every employee, our program will work." I said, "No. I'm not going to do that." They said, "Well, you're not going to do as well, but obviously we'll help you." Despite their warnings and complaints, we put in the program. Within two months there were some errors and many "innovations."

The program was based on Slack, and the employees received a monthly message on the platform for employees to click on a link to an article or video to learn about diversity. On paper, this was a great idea, but at the end of the day, everything is measured by execution. Over the next several months, there were minor errors and typical problems. Out of fairness to this vendor, some of the problems were typical glitches that come with any new platform.

Unfortunately, later there was a link sent out to all the employees with an article for them to read with some questions for discussion that some felt were offensive. This company was out of Canada, and their particular definitions of First Nations and People of Color were not quite the same. As a result, some felt offended because of how some of the questions were stated, and People of Color were completely left out. The company was very apologetic, but it was the kind of error that any US-based diversity officer would have caught. It is the kind of mistake you don't want to make early in establishing a new DE&I program. I am sure many of you are now wondering why I did not review it first. As I mentioned, what I have learned over the years is that new DE&I programs are under-resourced. I was a team of one, and you typically don't have bandwidth to catch everything. That is why I pilot programs, and I never put the CEO's endorsement on things too soon. I give vendors the time to prove themselves before sending out a companywide email from the CEO.

Most CEOs are going to tell you, "I'm not thin skinned. I understand things are going to happen. I wouldn't fly off the handle after one mistake." They're right. But you only get three strikes. Let's be honest about that, so don't launch your DE&I program on a mistake that could have been avoided. You don't want to use up one of your three strikes for a program you aren't sure about. That's why you don't ask for the CEO to use their position to encourage people to participate in diversity programs until after you've run some initiatives, there have been some pilots, and you've worked out the kinks. Don't go get CEO endorsement too early. Don't think every initiative has to have the CEO's endorsement on it because you've been told it's considered a "best practice," or the CEO has to be committed. That sounds great, but know when to get it, how to get it, and when to use it. That way, when you do ask for the CEO's time, they can be confident that you know what you're doing. You haven't embarrassed them, and you've put in programs that are going to work and be successful.

So how long do you have to wait until you connect the program to your CEO? Typically, I tell people, pilot your program for the first year. Once all the kinks are worked out, then you should have your CEO launch it, especially when it's a new initiative. Many times, when you start a new program where you're launching new initiatives, you'll have several that are launching at the same time. That's why I encourage you to pilot all of them, work out the kinks, and then that's when you do the full launch to make sure you have your CEO commitment. That way you're maximizing the leverage. You will look very polished, and people will respect the work that you are doing. It makes you look good. It makes the CEO look good. And your programs will be well-received.

Connecting CEO and Leadership Commitment to Diversity

Often diversity experts will tell you that compensation bonuses should be connected to diversity. Typically, there are no examples of how to do this, or they tie compensation directly to the percentage of diversity within the department. This can be very tricky because you need to understand the metrics and what leaders actually control. Without that understanding, leaders become quickly frustrated with DE&I goals that are tied to compensation because the goals are not achievable.

I typically do not tie compensation or bonuses to hiring goals because this method is fundamentally flawed. It is hard to predict the number of new hires or backfills. Additionally, a small number of hires can swing the percentages wildly. For example, you set a hiring target that 30% of all hires for the year should be People of Color. In this particular example, the leader had four opportunities to hire. This would mean they either miss the hiring target or blow right past it because statically you can be at zero or 25%, if you hire none or one Person of Color, so they miss the goal. The only other alternative is they end up at 50% or higher because any other hiring combination would put them over the goal. There is no doubt that 30% may be a reasonable hiring target, but there is no way to know in advance (when you set the goal) that four people were going to leave the organization, which throws off the target. You will also find a similar problem if you tie compensation to the diversity of the department. This is because in order to make a department more diverse, people have to leave. Leaders are tasked with keeping good people. If they are successful, they are limiting opportunities to make the department more diverse.

So what should the solution be? How do we hold leaders accountable by connecting DE&I to a compensation bonus? I recommend that leaders be held to hires, promotions, and terminations that reflect equity. So the metric to hiring is that individuals from underrepresented groups are hired at a rate that is equal to or greater than their availability in the market. The metric for promotions and terminations would be that individuals from underrepresented groups are at parity with their peers, meaning that, for example, individuals who identify as women in the engineering department receive promotions at the same rate as their peers who do not identify as women. We should also see the same thing with terminations. In the end, we would like to see that voluntary or involuntary terminations would be similar in rate.

Below you will find a leadership commitment matrix example that can be used for executive leaders' annual compensation/bonus. They can be asked to commit to support DE&I efforts via participation in three or four of the seven key activities. Holding them to this type of matrix will show the company leadership's DE&I commitment. The example of this matrix is shown in Figure 10.1.

A tool like this can help you start a discussion about what commitment looks like and what realistic expectations would be over a manageable timeframe. This is the best way to leverage CEO and senior leadership commitment and also make reasonable progress.

	Sample Leadership DE&I Commitment Compensation Matrix
1	Commit to use of the 4-2-50 process in hiring leaders in your respective division/department.
2	Participation and attendance at two or more Diversity, Equity, and Inclusion training sessions.
3	Participation of 50% or more of your staff at 75% of Diversity, Equity, and Inclusion Training sessions.
4	Participation and attendance at two or more ERG events during the year or serving as the executive leader advisor to an ERG.
5	Participation in an external organization that as its primary goal has the purposes of furthering Diversity, Equity, and Inclusion (Social Justice).
6	Percent of promotion of women and POC is equal to company average.
7	Retention of women and POC is equal to company average.

Figure 10.1 Sample Leadership for Diversity, Equity, and Inclusion Commitment.

How to Get CEO Commitment

When getting CEO commitment, it comes down to who, when, why, and how. CEO commitment is about these four simple questions. If you want CEO commitment, you need to be clear with them about: *Who* you need them to impact or influence, *when* to influence them, *why* they are asked to be involved, and *how* to use their position to make change.

The who you need the CEO to influence may seem obvious as we would hope they will impact all employees. This is true, but to be most impactful and effective, getting all leaders to actively support initiatives is most helpful. As I mentioned before, use your CAPE data to assist the CEO in holding the leadership team and others accountable to specific goals.

Let the CEO know *when* you need their influence, whether it be to launch a program or contact leaders. *When* is also knowing, as the DE&I leader, the best time to use the CEO's influence, as I explained earlier in this chapter. Putting the CEOs name on every DE&I program initiative launch is not a good idea.

Why CEO influence is important? The CEO's influence is needed to move the company toward their DE&I commitments. But it can be best done when you follow the principles of CAPE. You need the data to show which initiatives are essential for the organization, where the organization or departments started from, and why you are focusing your efforts to maximize resources and outcomes.

How you use the CEO's influence will be crucial to gain their trust and support for DE&I initiatives and programs. The *how* is also about giving the CEO the tools and the data they need, so they know how to support the DE&I program. It has to be more than just statements. The CEO can review the DE&I data with each leader, attend trainings, and set the tone in how they support you as a leader.

KEY POINTS

- Understand the importance of setting accurate and realistic expectations for the CEO and leaders.
- Don't go get CEO endorsement too early. Pilot your program for the first year.
- Use data to partner with the CEO and show them the *who, when, why*, and *how* to use their influence to move the DE&I program and meeting objectives.

Chapter 11

Employee Resource Groups

Check Your Bias

A couple of years ago, I was asked to be on a panel to discuss diversity, equity, and inclusion at a very successful tech company. The event was held at their recently built headquarters. The place was amazing! It had a coffee bar, a cafeteria with a sushi chef, meditation rooms, and every modern amenity that all tech companies instinctively know to include in their buildings.

After the panel, I was asked to meet with a small group of employees from diverse backgrounds. The employees of this tech company were in the process of attempting to start employee resource groups (ERGs) for employees from underrepresented groups. They told me they were getting a lot of pushback from company leaders. There were concerns that these groups were somehow self-segregating and might make some of the White males feel unwelcome. Moreover, they needed to give the management team the business case for ERGs. In this case it was ERGs for LGBTQ+, women, and People of Color that were organizing.

To answer the question of the business case for ERGs, I looked across the pristine lobby and pointed at the ping pong table and said, "What is the business case for that? And what was the business case for the coffee bar? Did anyone need to explain those items or sushi to the leadership team?"

This group of employees looked at me, and I did not have to say another word. They intuitively got the point I was making because tech company leaders rarely need the business case for ping pong tables or coffee bars. These are things companies provide to keep "good employees." It hadn't yet occurred to the leaders at this company that group meetings for employees from underrepresented groups is another thing that they could do to keep valued employees.

ERG meetings are open to anyone to attend. If it is a women's ERG, all women are *not* required to attend, and men are *not* prevented from attending. The basis of the ERG is that all participants have agreed that the intent of the meeting is to discuss issues and opportunities for women. It is just like the company softball team. If you go to the softball practice or game, everyone assumes you are there to play softball. It is not a group of people organizing against those that don't play softball.

As for the other part of the question, that ERGs might make White males feel uncomfortable, this is my request: Ask yourself what are you assuming about these groups? Why do you assume some negative intent?

Throughout my career, I have walked by many rooms full of employees, and I have never yet assumed they are segregating themselves or were up to something negative. In addition, it's not unusual for these groups of employees to be all White, or even all White and all male – but I do not assume they are self-segregating or have some negative goal.

When you see ERGs meeting, I ask you to check your bias. If you are thinking that you would not be welcome in the room or that the group is planning a coup, you are the problem. It is time for some self-evaluation. Check your bias.

What you are feeling or thinking when you see a room of Latinx employees has nothing to do with the group of people, and everything to do with the assumptions you are making about them. If your leadership team needs a business case for employees with a shared lived experience meeting together, ask them to check their bias. The company softball team is not for everyone, nor is the free coffee, or the ping pong table – yet they are provided. Accept a different reality.

I often hear that people should be allowed to bring their complete selves to work. In some cases, that might mean that they would like to meet with people who have a shared experience, including sometimes a shared struggle. The reality is that the world is still struggling with issues of race, gender, ability, sexual orientation, and other "isms." Ignoring that reality is not a solution.

Anytime you are faced with a group that isn't just like you, I ask you to check your bias and accept that some people have a different reality from yours. Some people want to play ping pong, some join the company softball team, and others meet in a room to discuss their shared experience. All of these activities keep good employees.

This chapter will take you through the pros and cons of ERGs. I'll provide insights about ERGs and decision-making, communication guidelines, and your role as the DE&I leader. I offer you some rules and structures to help organize ERGs and manage fundraisers. Last, and it may surprise you, we'll talk about when and why you might want to let a company ERG fail.

Employee Resource Groups

DE&I programs can be a heavy load. I have learned over the years of running DE&I programs that not everything gets fixed or has to be addressed. Some things will need to wait, and most importantly, if you carry the load yourself, it breaks you down.

For example, all DE&I programs have or develop employee resource groups (ERGs) or affinity groups. These groups are typically groups of employees that have organized around a shared experience, shared heritage, or a desire to learn and support one of these groups. An example can be a women's ERG, parents' ERG, Asian ERG, and so on. Often as the chief diversity officer, you feel responsible for these groups' success, and therefore attend every meeting and pick up any slack in the events.

You will also find that ERG members think you should be at every event or meeting. Many of the members will also be quick to point out to you if you are not at every meeting. This creates a lot of pressure externally and internally for you as the chief diversity officer (CDO). In the past, I have worked in organizations that have had 9 or 10 ERGs, so making every meeting is not a reasonable expectation.

The reality is that if you make every ERG meeting, participate in every hiring to ensure diversity, provide DE&I training, review all content, support the HR department with every personnel problem related to DE&I, and prepare the board report, you will be spread too thin. In addition, the racism, sexism, or other -isms that many employees come to you with can be something you yourself are experiencing.

Being the CDO can be very lonely. Some White employees feel as though you are not supporting them, and the DE&I training is not enough. Employees of Color feel as though you are not supporting them and will tell you the DE&I training is too slow and nothing is changing fast enough. As a result, no one is happy with your work.

Remember, what Lena Horne said, "It's not the load that breaks you down; it's the way you carry it." Give yourself permission to *not* make every ERG meeting, let some things wait for another day, and don't carry the load all by yourself. Delegate. Rely on friends, and if necessary, let some ERGs fail. So, let's look more closely at ERGs and how to lighten your load.

Define ERG Membership

Working with ERGs or affinity groups can be fun but exhausting if not managed well. They can be a great way to retain employees and can help support diversity-focused initiatives. They are very useful internal focus groups and tend to be underutilized by most companies in that capacity. I would caution that they can be overutilized when they are used as a less-expensive alternative to hiring and fully supporting a DE&I program. Women, People of Color, persons with disabilities, or LGBTQ+ employees should not be tasked with DE&I in addition to their jobs.

ERGs become challenging because they are a best practice. By that I mean that everyone thinks a company should have them, but rarely do you find any information on how to create guidelines for ERGs or on what the ERGs can and cannot achieve.

I always tell people the job of the diversity officer, when it comes to ERGs, is to support when needed and be the referee. Typically, what you will find is that something happens where there is a disagreement or question about procedure, and they need someone to enforce the rules. So, if you have good ERG guidelines in the beginning, it makes it easier to manage the ERGs later. Guidelines help you, for example, if someone gets elected to lead the group, but they stop coming to meetings and stop fulfilling the responsibilities of the position, there is a process to replace the person. The guidelines will be the fundamental rules that all employees agreed they would play by. I have shared a set of ERG guidelines as an example later in this chapter.

Something that will be of paramount importance for managing and leading ERGs is to know when an employee is a member of an ERG and when they are not. The point here is this: ERGs typically like to do some socializing. For example, years ago, I had an ERG decide they would have a tailgating party to support the local college team. The issue with events like tailgating is that people drink alcohol. Then afterward, everyone says, "Oh, this was so much fun. We had a great time. Why don't we go as a group to the bar and have some drinks?" And I always say, it is important to let everyone know that when they are drinking alcohol in a public establishment, they are no longer your employees. So, in this example, the guidelines for the ERGs need to make sure they distinguish when someone is an employee and when they are not an employee, but a customer of the bar. I would discourage tailgating as an ERG event for this reason. They can still get together, but they are meeting as friends and not as the ERG.

This event also highlighted another ERG challenge people don't often think about. For the tailgating party, everyone in the ERG wanted to wear a T-shirt to support the local college with a logo from the school and a logo from our company. This can create several challenges. First, typically you will need to get approval from both the local team and your organization. If you don't already have a relationship with the college and permission to use the logo, you will need to get approval. You will more than likely also need to get approval from your company to use the logo. Getting logo permission can be difficult, and it can take time to get all the necessary approvals. ERGs sometimes don't follow the process, and if those unauthorized T-shirts get printed, it is your fault because you are the diversity officer.

Setting up ERG guidelines is something no one ever tells you about when managing an ERG program, but you have to do this and make sure that everyone understands. Guidelines need to cover a variety of situations. This includes things like:

- ERG don't represent the organization.
- ERGs cannot sign an agreement on behalf of the organization.
- ERGs need company approval to use the logo or brand.
- ERGs are not decision-making organizations for the company.

I would strongly encourage you to have the ERG guidelines reviewed by the legal department and/or outside counsel. Generally, it is good to include a statement that reminds members of the ERG that they are required to understand and follow the standards of professionalism and behavior as outlined in the employee handbook.

ERGs sometimes blur the line between employee and public citizen. I am not discounting how important it is to network and develop professional relationships, but you need to be clear there are times when socializing is not part of an ERG's work.

Setting Boundaries for ERGs

Employees sometimes think the ERGs are going to set up initiatives, do outreach, and represent the company at events. They may want to start a community initiative or create a partnership with a local nonprofit. These initiatives need to be approved by your company with the appropriate departments included and with appropriate expectations for what can be achieved.

This is not to minimize the work ERGs can do or their importance, but many times if you don't specify their role and limitations, the ERG may do things with which the organization may not agree, and as the DE&I officer, you will be held responsible. For example, what if the ERG goes to a political rally to support a local or national candidate. Typically, organizations try to stay out of elections, but now you're at odds with the ERG, which has given the appearance that the company is supporting a candidate, and the company leadership is blaming you because you are the sponsor of the company ERGs. To prevent this from happening, make sure to clearly articulate your policy in the guidelines.

Then the ERG members will understand that the ERG is not a decision-making organization, the members cannot represent the company, and they cannot create partnerships for the company.

Even what may appear to be a simple initiative with great intentions can become troublesome. For example, an ERG may want to create a recruitment/mentorship effort to increase the number of Students of Color from the local college in the accounting department. This is probably something that needs to be done, but that recruitment effort is the job of the recruiters, the diversity officer, and the company's accounting department leaders. (Needless to say, this is a decision that also needs to be based on the CAPE data collection and analysis.) Often, I have found this creates several problems, one of which could be that there is already a partnership or one being developed by the organization/company. Now you have two different people from the same company contacting the college. It goes without saying this is not a great look.

It's also important to remember that ERG members are volunteers. What happens if a few members take opportunities at other companies? What if a few members are promoted and now have less bandwidth? The remaining members lose energy for this initiative, and all of sudden you are running the ERG's recruitment program to save relationships and the image of the company. DE&I programs and initiatives need to have *company* support, resources, and staff, not just ERG support for this very reason.

Another reason to limit the ERGs' ability to create partnerships is to preserve the coordination of company efforts. Coordination is important for DE&I initiatives that have external partnerships, and this should be done by the larger organization with the necessary understanding of the company's strategy and vision. The last thing you want to happen is to have to redirect the limited resources and budget of your DE&I department to save a program that was not well planned out and is not aligned with the overall company DE&I commitments. ERG members, despite their best intentions, are often not equipped to plan, launch, and run new company initiatives. That is why it is important to understand the level of coordination needed to have a highly functioning ERG program – and to place limits on the ERGs' role.

Make sure the ERGs know they cannot negotiate or create partnerships on behalf of the organization. This can be done without limiting their creativity. But the fact of the matter is, the last thing you want to happen is to have people represent themselves on behalf of the organization when they are not empowered to do so.

Establish Communication Guidelines

To maximize the effectiveness of ERG communications, you will need to set up some guidelines, so that all forms of messaging to all staff or external audiences require preapproval and are limited. This is important in the case that an ERG wants to send an email to all the employees to let them know about their upcoming event. For example, the Latinx ERG will want to send out invitations and information about Hispanic Heritage Month, which runs from September 15 to October 15. This makes perfect sense and should be done. However, the challenge is created because National Disability Employment Awareness Month is the month of October and the Persons with Disabilities ERG will also want to send out information about their planned events. Toward the end of October, the Native American and Indigenous People ERG may want to send out emails announcing events for the National Native American Heritage Month, which is November. One can quickly understand there could be a lot of company emails going out over a three- or four-week period. In some cases, there could be emails going out two or three times a week, and this will become too much for most employees and the discussion becomes about the volume of emails and not the events. The volume of emails or other forms of communication is often overlooked or minimized, but you would be surprised about how quickly volume will become an issue.

In order to avoid situations like this, create communications guidelines. In the guidelines, be clear that the ERGs cannot send any direct messaging (e.g., emails) or make a social media page (like Facebook) for the ERG. Any and all communications will need to be approved by the DE&I and/or communication department (marketing or the department that manages social media) prior to sending anything out to employees. Any and all forms of ERG communication should come from the DE&I department. Similarly, the DE&I department should manage all forms of social media. The last thing you want is a social media post on the company's ERG page that you cannot remove because you do not have the password and the ERG's former social media manager took a new job six weeks ago.

ERGs are going to want to get the word out about their events, so to support the ERGs and inform employees, I recommend preparing a monthly newsletter and an intranet landing page for all ERGs. Additionally, you can create a link to a place where employees can sign up to receive email directly from the ERGs. This will be the right balance for direct communication to employees because they have signed up for these direct emails and can ask to be removed.

Hopefully, your company has a communications or marketing person that will help you write a monthly newsletter and update the intranet landing page as a solution for these communication issues. (Yes, writing newsletters and updating websites is another skill diversity officers need to have, which no one tells you about.) Additionally, the person from communication/marketing can help to ensure all forms of messaging are in alignment with established employee non-solicitation and other communication policies for employees.

Managing ERG Fundraisers

Generally, I recommend that all fundraisers that are done by ERGs may only be for nonprofit organizations or foundations where the funds raised by the individual ERG member go directly to the nonprofit or foundation. This is for many reasons. First, if there are 50 members of the ERG and they raise $10,000, it is unreasonable to ask any one member of the ERG to hold the money. Additionally, for example, if there is a disagreement about a $500 cash donation, it becomes an impossible situation for you to mediate. You do not want to be in the situation of making a decision or mediating whether the $500 cash donation was, or was not, made and who actually received it. Setting up a bank account for the ERG at the local back is not an option because the ERG will need to use the company Tax ID or someone's personal information. Needless to say, sharing the company Tax ID is not a good idea. Using an employee's name and personal information is a worse idea because if that employee leaves the company or something unpredictable happens to them, you may never get access to the account.

The solution here is to budget some dollars in the DE&I program so that the ERGs can apply for funding of their events on an annual basis. Inform the ERGs that the use of the funds will have to be consistent with the company expense policies. This keeps the DE&I program out of any questions about appropriate use, and employees typically already understand the expense policy.

The limitation on fundraising should also extend to donations of items. I would recommend that any donated items be done in a way that each ERG member is participating by taking items directly to the nonprofit or foundation. ERGs should not set up a system where the members take the items to be stored in an employee's garage for any period of time. One simple reason is, what if on the day the items need to be delivered, the person holding the items is unavailable? How do you get into the garage? Additionally, this can create some potential liabilities to the employee and company that are not worth the risk. If the donation of items is part of a larger company-wide initiative and the company has a space to keep the items, that would be a much better solution.

ERG fundraisers need to be carried out in a manner consistent with the company solicitation policy. Typically, most organizations have limitations on, or policies about, asking for funds or donations from its employees. So, make sure you make reference to that in your ERG guidelines.

Let ERGs Fail

One surprising thing that I always tell people is that it is okay to let ERGs fail. Over the years, I have received many calls from DE&I professionals with questions about how to save an ERG. They will tell me things like, "There is low attendance," and "No one will do anything." I will tell them to let the ERG fail. That is typically not what people want to hear, but as I mentioned, DE&I programs have limited bandwidth and need to maximize resources. There is no need to have an ERG that is not functioning or has no attendance to keep going. For example, if there is an ERG for young leaders, and nobody is coming to the meetings, do not feel obligated to save the ERG. It could be there is no interest from employees in the ERG. What I have found is that diversity directors run themselves ragged by coordinating all the meetings and setting up all the agendas to try to keep the ERG alive. As a diversity officer with a limited budget, limited staff, and four or five different initiatives, what you don't want is to be running three ERGs all the time too.

Another reason, I tell DE&I leaders to let ERGs fail is so that those employees who believe the ERGs are important will step up. If no one steps up, then you should let it fail because there are no employees who are interested in it. Remember ERGs can be started again later. You need to let those processes happen because that is part of the learning process, and you want to empower employees to run the ERG. You will wear yourself ragged if you run every ERG and never allow them to fail. And there are so many different things that have to be done. So, my advice is to put together good fundamental rules and allow ERGs to flourish or fail.

The How: Suggested Rules and Structures for ERGs

ERGs can be very supportive of your DE&I initiatives and will be a great resource for the organization. So, the point here is not to say don't create ERGs; it's that you need to create some good fundamental guidelines so that you can prevent future headaches (and lighten your load). Up to this point, I have outlined some of the bigger challenges that you may face when you are responsible for the company's ERGs. To help ERGs get started on the right foot and/or support their continued success, here are additional guidelines I would recommend:

- **Limit terms.** You do not want a situation where you have one person who is always the chair of the ERG. One of the goals for the ERGs is to cultivate and develop leadership skills, and that can't happen if you always have the same leader. Limit leadership positions to no more than two years. Anything beyond that is going to create problems because other employees get frustrated when there are no opportunities to lead, and then you end up managing personalities around the ERG rather than having ERGs that support the company's mission for diversity.
- **Assign an executive sponsor.** Do not put the ERGs in a situation where they have to approach individual company leaders and ask them to become the ERG sponsor. The DE&I office should request

volunteers and be the one to ask the company executives to be a sponsor. This prevents awkwardness about an executive needing to say no. The company executive may not have the bandwidth to be the sponsor, but saying no could be perceived as being unsupportive of diversity or the particular ERG.

Figure 11.1 is a sample set of ERG general guidelines. Feel free to tweak as necessary for your organization, but be sure to incorporate all the important guidelines discussed previously.

SAMPLE GUIDELINES FOR EMPLOYEE RESOURCE GROUPS

Employee Resource Groups (ERGs) are company sponsored and voluntary associations of people with common interests. ERGs are open to full-time and part-time [COMPANY] employees. [COMPANY] related ERGs are designed to increase employee engagement and develop a higher performing workforce.

Purpose of Employee Resource Groups

A fundamental requirement of all ERGs is to promote the mission of [COMPANY] and to establish mutually beneficial relationships between [COMPANY], its workforce, and members of the Employee Resource Group. It is important to have resource groups that are tailored to the needs of [COMPANY] and to make certain that these groups are inclusive for everyone. The goal of an ERG is to develop an environment of respect and inclusion in an effort to enhance [COMPANY's] culture for employees:

- Increase awareness of issues as they relate to diversity, equity, and inclusion in [COMPANY] culture.
- Provide a forum for the open candid exchange of information and ideas and its relation to the workplace.
- Provide resources and assistance in implementing [COMPANY] diversity strategy through participation in recruitment, retention, and community outreach initiatives.
- Strengthen relationships to diverse communities.
- Positively impact the surrounding community.

Figure 11.1 Sample Guidelines for ERG.

ERG Expectations

ERGs are expected to promote [COMPANY's] broader mission, goals, and values.

Establishing an Employee Resource Group

Employees wishing to form an ERG should contact the diversity, equity, and inclusion vice president or Human Resources. The (ADD THE COMPANY dept. here) is responsible for general oversight and administration of the ERG program. Sponsorship of ERGs is subject to review and approval by (COMPANY diversity, equity, and inclusion department). Each group will be required to:

- Develop a mission statement or statement of purpose that links the group's mission to [COMPANY's] mission and values;
- Create by-laws, that will define the leadership, election process, and membership criteria;
- Identify specific areas for activity that are relevant to the group's constituency;
- Define the group's leadership and membership structure;
- Identify metrics to assess the impact of the group's work and report semi-annually to the group's executive sponsor and to the diversity and inclusion department.

Executive sponsors should be either at the VP or director level. The job of the sponsor is to keep the ERG focused on business goals; however the sponsor should *not* be one of the group's direct leaders.

Company Support to Established ERGs

[COMPANY] will provide the following support to sponsored ERGs:

1. An executive sponsor will be assigned to each ERG. This sponsor will advise and assist the group's members on aligning their activities with [COMPANY's] values, goals, business practices, and objectives.
2. With prior approval company-sponsored ERGs may use company facilities for meetings.
3. A company-sponsored ERG will receive guidance and support from the diversity, equity, and inclusion program to establish the group's goals and objectives, infrastructure, and operating procedures.

Figure 11.1 (*Continued*)

4. ERGs may receive limited financial support to cover the group's routine expenses, including but not limited to printing, refreshments, and speaker fees by submitting the appropriate forms to [COMPANY] DE&I program. The DE&I program is responsible for reviewing and approving all requests. [COMPANY] is not responsible for any financial obligation or any other type of liability incurred by an ERG; those are the responsibility of the group's officers and members.

5. [COMPANY] dollars are not to be used for items, events, or activities that are purely recreational, limited in benefit, and/or do not meet the larger objective of promoting the mission of [COMPANY] and to establish mutually beneficial relationships between [COMPANY], its workforce, and members of the Employee Resource Group.

Guiding Principles of Established ERGs

1. An ERG is a voluntary organization that must be open to all full- and part-time regular employees. Temporary employees, contractors, vendors, or other non-employees are not eligible for membership in an ERG.

2. It is expected that all members of an ERG and participants in any ERG meeting, event, or activity will observe the general standards of professionalism as detailed in [COMPANY] Employee Handbook and Code of Conduct.

3. ERGs do *not* represent individuals or groups in their relationship with [COMPANY]. Employees who have concerns about specific issues raised within an ERG or by themselves (including wages, hours, and conditions of employment) should address them through available formal communication processes or directly to Human Resources.

4. Each ERG is responsible for the communications it disseminates. The content of these communications must comply with the general standards of professionalism, all [COMPANY] policies and code of conduct and be consistent with [COMPANY's] interest in promoting inclusion, equal opportunity, and diversity in the workplace within the context of the company's mission, values, and business objectives.
   - Communications must clearly identify the ERG as a voluntary organization of individuals who are [COMPANY] employees, and not as a [COMPANY] business organization.
   - ERGs may not present themselves as representing [COMPANY] or as expressing the view of [COMPANY].

Figure 11.1 (Continued)

- A copy of all communication material must first be approved by [COMPANY] director of communications. Once approved, it must be sent to the group's executive sponsor and to the diversity, equity, and inclusion department.
- ERGs may not use non-[COMPANY]-maintained media for the dissemination of information. This includes social media sites, such as Facebook and Twitter, blogs, websites, newsletters, magazines, and newspapers.

5. With prior approval from [COMPANY], the company's e-mail and internal mail system may be used by ERGs for communications with members, subject to compliance with [COMPANY's] guidelines governing such use. Mass mailings or emails to non-members and/or subsets of the entire staff who are not members need approval from the executive sponsor, communications, and DE&I program.

Adherence to [COMPANY] Standards

ERG members must:

- Conduct themselves and their activities in accordance with **all [COMPANY] policies and [COMPANY] code of conduct.**
- Ensure that any time spent on ERG activities does not reduce business productivity or negatively impact job performance and is supported by their direct supervisor.

Employee Resource Groups and employees who violate corporate standards or any policies may lose company privileges, and may be subject to discipline up to and including termination of employment. [COMPANY] may cease its support of an ERG at any time for any reason.

Employee Resource Group Operating Principles

1. Members must be employed by [COMPANY].
2. The formation of the Employee Resource Group must rely on volunteers, and neither [COMPANY] nor members of the group may pressure any employee into joining.
3. Membership in an Employee Resource Group shall be entirely voluntary.

Figure 11.1 (Continued)

4. The Employee Resource Group should be organized to assist and support the [COMPANY]'s mission by hosting activities, such as the following:
   a. Community relations programs
   b. Promoting social and intellectual enrichment
   c. Networking opportunities
   d. Providing alternative educational and civic activities deemed to be beneficial to the membership of the Employee Resource Group
5. Employee Resource Groups are encouraged to collaborate to the maximum extent feasible to facilitate understanding between groups and to maximize resources for the benefit or each group.
6. ERG meetings can be held during work hours, but employee participation at these meeting is with the supervisor's permission.
7. Exempt employees attending an event or volunteer hours at events outside of normal business hours will not be compensated.
8. Up to 10% of an employee's goals can be directly related to a leadership position within the ERG if the employee has been asked by [COMPANY] leadership to assume the role with supervisor's consent. Leadership roles are limited to the positions defined with in the ERG bylaws.

Figure 11.1 (Continued)

JASON-ISM

ERGs can be your best friend or your worst headache. Learn to use them to lighten your load.

One of my most painful memories is being on a panel with two individuals who were new diversity officers. We were asked to answer a simple question: "How do you handle stress?" When the question about stress came to the person seated immediately next to me, they said, "My only goal [is] to answer this question without crying." Then, they began crying as soon as the words left their mouth. You may not be able to change the load, but don't let how you carry it break you down. How you carry the load is the only thing you can control. ERGs can help to carry the load with you, or they can break you down if you try to be all things to all people all of the time.

KEY POINTS

- ERG meetings are open to anyone to attend. The basis of the ERG is that all participants have agreed that the intent of the meeting is to discuss issues and opportunities for a particular group.
- Use ERGs to help you carry the load of retaining a diverse workforce, but do not feel pressure to attend every ERG meeting.
- It is okay to let ERGs fail.
- Set clear guidelines for ERGs and establish that ERGs are not decision-making bodies for the company.
- Ask the legal department or an outside attorney to review the ERG guidelines if necessary.

Chapter 12

DE&I Committees

Focus on the Right Things

Recently my spouse and I sat down to watch a video of our kids when they were very young. In the video I think Justus was barely four, and Piper was not quite two. Amazing as it sounds, it was the first time I had really seen Piper's hair.

For years whenever we discussed Piper as a small infant or toddler, we would say, "Poor Piper did not have any hair until she was almost four!" We would go on and on about how wonderful it was when she finally had enough hair to put it in a ponytail. You see Piper's hair was very thin and wispy and could not be combed or brushed. My mother would tell us that we should comb it and instruct us in how my brother would blow-dry his daughter's hair straight. My mom would imply that the only real problem with Piper's hair was that her parents would not take the time to blow-dry and comb "poor" Piper's hair. I remember how my wife and I would lament about what to do with Piper's hair before every trip to my parents' house. At that time my parents lived about a 10-minute drive from our home, and we saw them every week. Piper's hair became quite an issue. We would try to comb it, but it was no use. In fact, even Piper would say, "I have crazy hair." Our only relief from Grandma's suggestion that all Piper's hair needed was a blow-dry came one day when we left Piper at Grandma's house and went shopping for about two hours. As soon as my wife and I got back to Grandma's house and saw Piper, we both smiled with quiet satisfaction. Piper's hair was going in every direction in a very bizarre looking afro. Grandma had tried to blow-dry and comb Piper's hair. We knew right away what Grandma had done because we had tried to blow-dry Piper's crazy hair on several occasions and had gotten the same result. After that even Grandma would say, "Piper has crazy hair!"

Things finally reached a pinnacle when Piper was almost four. One day, Justus came home from school and said, "Tomorrow is crazy hair day at school, and there is a contest to see who has the craziest hair." The whole family became depressed, finally a competition that Piper could win with her crazy hair, but she was too young to participate! Piper was still in preschool! Not only did Piper have crazy hair, but bad luck too! I can vividly remember when Piper finally had enough hair for a ponytail. We could not wait to get to Grandma's house to show her. Piper no longer had crazy hair.

So, it was funny watching that video years later, when I realized that Piper had never had "crazy hair." Piper's hair was absolutely beautiful. It was perfect. It was thin, wispy, and curly in the cutest way possible. It fit every part of Piper's personality. I remember looking at my wife while watching that video, and I could tell my wife had the same thought in her head "What a lost opportunity!" We should have spent more time enjoying that perfect hair. We should not have worried about what other people were thinking and truly enjoyed that wonderful hair. It is funny how many opportunities are lost in life because we worry too much about what others might think. We can't enjoy a meal there tonight because of what others might think of our clothes, I can't date him or her because of what others might think, we have to do it because of what will others think. And the list goes on and on.

The real question should be, how will this situation/experience/ encounter make my life and those around me better? It is amazing how many decisions we make are based on what we think others are thinking, rather than on what we know. I don't actually know what people thought of Piper's hair, but I know I wasted too much time worrying about it. What a shame! Piper's hair was always beautiful, and I should have enjoyed it. I was too worried about what others might think, and that was not something I could change. I was focused on the wrong things and missed an opportunity.

Piper, I hope you read this and when you do, know that you are all things beautiful, inside and out. Your hair, your brown skin, your laugh, your love for life, *you* are now and will always be Piper and perfect in every way. I love you.

In this chapter, I share what I have found working with DE&I committees. They often struggle because, like my story, they are focused on the wrong things instead of what they can actually change. DE&I programs have very broad responsibilities, and there is pressure to fix everything at once, and the pressure can become overwhelming. I will outline the reasons why DE&I committees fail, and I will present some options for how you can make your committee successful. Ultimately, successful DE&I committees and leaders can't spend too much time worrying about what others think. I encourage you to stay in the moment. DE&I is a journey; enjoy the moment, and take the wins when they come.

Why DE&I Committees Fail

DE&I committees are typically created to lead or support the DE&I program, while ERGs are primarily focused on the shared experience and support of their members. For example, an ERG could be a group of Asian employees that focus on conversations and events focused on Asian culture. In contrast, a DE&I committee is going to be focused on everything related to diversity, equity, and inclusion for the entire company. Sometimes they exist to lead the DE&I efforts instead of hiring a DE&I leader. DE&I committees are not a good alternative to hiring a DE&I professional. I can tell you the way I got two of my last three jobs was because the company started with a DE&I committee and quickly figured out they needed to hire someone. Like ERGs, diversity committees are popular, but they, too, have their pitfalls.

DE&I committees can prove to be helpful to company DE&I programs, but in full transparency, it is because of their weaknesses that I was recruited to launch DE&I programs. Generally, what happens is that a group of employees will get together as the DE&I committee and make a big list of programs, initiatives, and ideas. One of the weaknesses is that everyone generally understands diversity, equity, and inclusion, so the assumption is anyone can do it. The reality is that things don't get done because the goals are too big or because they are not executable in the set timeline. The major weakness is that everyone on the DE&I committee is a volunteer and has a primary job responsibility that is not DE&I. If no one is directly responsible for DE&I program tasks and everyone is a volunteer, generally very few things ever get done. One obvious reason for this is because employees prioritize the job they have been hired for first. This generally takes time, so DE&I projects get pushed back. In the end, the members of the committee will come to the conclusion that the company needs to hire someone.

If you think about it logically, creating a committee to run a major initiative in a company would not be considered a good idea. For example, everyone uses money and has for the most part worked in a company that had money. All employees have some amount of money that they spend, save, and understand how to use. So, why not get rid of the accounting department and have everyone be responsible for the company's expenditures and the collection of money? Shouldn't the company just create a committee to meet once a month? That should be enough, and it would save money too. Of course, no company would agree to this because accounting is a primary function, and you need expertise to be an accountant. Unfortunately, the logic for diversity is that anyone can do it, so just use volunteers. If the company uses a committee to do DE&I instead of hiring an expert, it speaks to their lack of commitment.

Another reason I have found that DE&I committees fail is because they are not really empowered to make decisions, and they do not have the necessary resources to implement a program. There is no real budget, no staff to do the day-to-day work, and the things they can impact change slowly because they simply don't have the authority to make the desired change. For example, implementing DE&I training sounds like a simple idea, but who is going to do the actual training? How do you pay the trainer if you use an outside vendor? What budget does the money for training come from? Is the training coordinated with the HR staff? Generally, companies like to keep track of who has participated in the training. Can any of the members of the committee get the data on who participated in the training, and are members allowed to see the data? Setting up what would appear to be a simple program becomes much more complicated, and members only see slow movement. As a result, people get frustrated, and they stop showing up to committee meetings. So again, running a DE&I program with solely a DE&I committee typically does not set you up for success.

DE&I work should not be approached as a hobby for employees with free time. What happens is that people get busy with their primary job responsibilities, whether in accounting, sales, or management. Sure, diversity is important to them, but they must do their accounting job first because that's what they are being paid for. Therefore, the committee's diversity initiatives keep getting pushed down farther and farther, and they always become a secondary priority.

The other piece is that generally committees don't have any positional authority, so they can't make change. Maybe the committee thinks the marketing department should do more about diversity and how we present our company to the world. The marketing department may or may not do it. Why? The committee has no positional authority.

The reality is that diversity, equity, and inclusion are complicated and require expertise. Having experienced racism does not make you an expert in all forms of discrimination, any more than having had an appendectomy makes you a doctor.

What Happens When Companies *Start* with a DE&I Committee

DE&I committees always sound like a great thing to start with for a company, rather than hire a full-time chief diversity officer. I have often heard that if you want to do diversity, equity, and inclusion, just have the company get a committee together. And, generally, what happens is company leaders get together and think, "Shouldn't everyone do diversity? We all think this is important. Why don't we just put together a committee?" In theory, this sounds like a great idea. Generally, committees don't execute. And the reason is simple. It's not their job.

They don't tell you this, but to start as the chief diversity officer of a diversity program when the committee already exists is difficult. It becomes a power struggle between you and the committee. Because the committee existed before you were hired, they have been led to believe they are running things and that your job is to respond to the committee and whoever you report to in the organization.

This presents a situation where you have eight bosses (or whatever the number of committee members may be), all of whom think they are there to tell you what to do. They're not. And if you disagree, they outvote you. To remove any unnecessary conflict, diversity committees are best established after the DE&I leader is hired. I have generally found that these committees create more frustration than solutions, both for the members of the committee and the DE&I leader, as I have outlined above. They don't work well in most organizations, although they have been recommended as a best practice. In general, there are no committees for other departments in a company because it rarely makes things more efficient or successful.

Diversity committees are also often created as a response to an issue, and the company often puts the committee in place before they hire people to work on diversity. In this situation, you have diversity committee members who have already set up goals and objectives. They may have had great ideas, but those ideas may not always be where you want to start or what you want to prioritize.

Three Simple Rules for a Better DE&I Committee

Regardless of when or why the diversity committee was created, here are some general recommendations on how to best structure the DE&I committee for success. Be sure to outline and define decisions and parameters around these key areas. The three areas I would recommend that you make sure are very clearly spelled out are listed in Figure 12.1.

Recommendation number one is to clearly define that the DE&I leader will make decisions, and the DE&I committee will make recommendations. This is going to be of paramount importance. Everyone needs to understand that the DE&I strategy and vision are set by the organizational leaders, not by the committee. This includes decision-making on the day-to-day workings of the DE&I program, reviewing employee data, and the recruitment and retention efforts that will be implemented by the DE&I leader. A place where a DE&I committee can make recommendations could be from a list of speakers/trainers you have provided. The committee members could also ask for financial

THREE RULES FOR A BETTER DIVERSITY COMMITTEE
DECISION-MAKING: Decisions are made by the DE&I leader. The DE&I committee makes recommendations.
BUDGET CONTROL: The DE&I committee does not have budget control.
LIST THINGS FOR THEM TO DO: The DE&I leader should list specific items the DE&I committee can implement.

Figure 12.1 Rules for a Better DE&I Committee.

support from the department they work in to bring in a major speaker or to identify ways to increase attendance at events. Just like any other department within the company, decisions are not made by a group of individuals from across the organization.

Recommendation number two, and this is a big one, *all* budget decisions need to be made by the DE&I leader. This rule needs to be made very clear to the committee. Marketing or IT does not use a committee to develop or make decisions about their budget, nor should DE&I.

Recommendation number three, the DE&I leader will outline tasks for the committee to do. For example, a lot of times people think, "Oh, we should have a resource of diversity information for employees to access." That is a great project for a diversity committee to work on. Because there are several members, who in their free time, can look for content. They can identify articles, books, and YouTube videos. They can help you work through those articles, help you narrow them down, or even interview potential speakers. This will be a great resource to have, and employees will use it. Also, you typically don't have the kind of time to build this resource, as it tends to be a lower priority. But if eight people work on it as a project, they can update it, feel good about what they have created, and if some things don't get done, you are not worse off. It's a win for everyone. They should be there to help you lighten the load.

As an added bonus, this is a task that is measurable. An employee DE&I resource site can be measured as to whether it was completed, and on an ongoing basis you can measure how much content is added and how often it is accessed. Another good project for a diversity committee could be organizing monthly DE&I trainings and speakers. The diversity committee can do the logistics of identifying speakers and create a list of trainings. That way, they're more apt to come back to committee meetings because now they have something specific to do as a diversity committee member.

You want to avoid a situation where the DE&I committee is randomly doing everything, and giving *you* projects to execute. If you get nothing else from this chapter, remember that the DE&I committee is not choosing how to prioritize work in the DE&I program or making decisions for you. DE&I committee members may believe they set the priorities and budget, but they should not. By establishing who makes budget and department decisions, you will save a lot of time and make the committee (and yourself) more effective.

JASON-ISM
DE&I committees work for you, not the other way around.

Remember, a diversity committee that has specific jobs to focus on will generally be more productive and positive. So, give your committee the job to organize diversity training. Make them responsible for that piece of DE&I. You put together a diversity calendar of trainings, and the diversity committee works on identifying what your trainings should be. That way, they're more apt to come back because they have something specific to do. That's the other thing people don't tell you about a diversity committee: many times they're doing something so broad that nothing happens. People keep showing up to meetings, and then everybody's frustrated. If you give them something to do, a very definitive task, everybody's going to be a lot happier. To be successful, create a committee that's responsible for well-defined, measurable tasks.

KEY POINTS

- DE&I committees are not a good alternative to hiring a DE&I professional because the members are volunteers who have their primary job as their priority, and the committees have no positional authority to effect change.
- DE&I committees can help you lighten the load, if the committee is organized accordingly.
- The three rules of an effective DE&I committee are: Establish the DE&I officer as the decision maker; clarify that the DE&I officer is in charge of the budget; and give the committee specific tasks that they can reasonably work on.

Chapter 13

Using DE&I Training to Make Organizational Change

Trees Just Don't Happen

I love trees. Several years ago, my spouse and I went through the process of buying a home. One of the things we both decided was that a must-have for our new home was trees. We wanted trees and never gave any thought to who planted them or how they got there. We just wanted a treed lot and were eventually able to buy the home with the trees we wanted.

While thinking about this recently I was reminded of something that happened a couple of years ago. I attended a viewing of the movie *Waiting for Superman* with the teachers from the Stanley Hupfeld Academy (SHA). The SHA is a charter school that serves a low-income population of students with all of the challenges you would expect from that environment. (I was at one point mentoring a child at SHA who confided in me that he was not eating on the weekends.)

153

Waiting for Superman is a documentary about the state of education in the United States. After the movie, there was a discussion about the current state of education in the United States. There were teachers in the theater from local charter schools from around the city in addition to the teachers from the Stanley Hupfeld Academy. The comments from the teachers covered a wide range of issues, but most of them felt a sincere concern about how to improve education in the United States.

About halfway into the discussion, a teacher from the Stanley Hupfeld Academy, said, "My students leave here and go to the Kipp Academy and do better. Maybe if they knew they had to perform to stay, they would do better for me. They get C's and D's with me and go to the KIPP Academy and get straight A's."

The thought in my head at that time was, "The students from SHA get A's at the Kipp Academy because you have prepared them to get A's." I have seen you hug these kids just because, challenge them to do better, and make them smile because you can. I imagine for many of these kids if you did not hug them, they would not be getting any hugs from an adult or any reassurance that things will be okay. Your compassion and desire to see them succeed is planting the seed. These students may not get A's with you, but they would not be getting A's if you had not taught them to read and write. If you had not helped them keep it together when their world was falling apart, they could not have develop into a successful student at the Kipp Academy.

It is hard being an elementary school teacher because when teaching is done well, the child assumes she did everything on her own. Good elementary teachers teach children to read and write, but most importantly, they build the confidence to learn. A good elementary teacher convinces the child that they can do it on their own. The child will not connect that passing a tough biology class in high school is directly related to learning to read in elementary school. Reading is a skill you learned in elementary school and the foundation for all the learning you will achieve for the rest of your life. Learning to read is planting the seed for future success.

The children from SHA did better at the Kipp Academy because of their teachers at SHA, not despite their best efforts. (I don't say this to take anything away from the Kipp Academy but to validate the commitment of the teachers at the Stanley Hupfeld Academy and many other committed elementary teachers.) I, like most people, love the trees, but I never think about who planted the seed. We can all enjoy the shade of a tree or the turning of the leaves in the fall, but few of us see who planted the seed. Trees just don't happen.

In this chapter you will learn the difference between DE&I trainings as episodes and DE&I trainings as a series. I'll also talk about how to do DE&I training with some tips and recommendations so that you can maximize their effectiveness, based on what your company needs most. The DE&I training you choose to offer needs to be based on data, and your goal should be to plant the DE&I seeds in the right places.

Diversity Training: Episode versus Series

Just like the trees in my blog, you have to plant seeds of diversity, equity, and inclusion in your company. What does this mean? Most times, it means diversity training of some sort. But what is the best way to do diversity training? This question actually comes up all the time, and quite frankly I can tell you that most people approach diversity training the wrong way.

Historically, diversity training is seen as a fully encapsulated answer in and of itself that can be used as a tool for any incidents of discrimination. If there was any episode of discrimination, simply reach for a mandatory DE&I training. But this approach doesn't work. We know this because we still have many episodes of discrimination against the LGBTQ community, against the communities with disabilities, and against People of Color. Racism, sexism, or any other -isms are part of a system or series of connected events. They are not episodic. DE&I training can have longer-term impact and create change if it is seen as a part of a response to a systemic problem instead of to a single episode of intolerance that one might consider an anomaly, thereby ignoring systemic biases.

> **JASON-ISM**
> We must begin doing DE&I training as a response to an ongoing series of connected events and not as a response to unconnected episodes or events. Solutions to systemic discrimination have to look like the recurring problem – not one time training.

Racism and sexism have long complicated histories in the United States. They are systemic and institutionalized. This has been well documented and is considered a matter of record. I would encourage you to read *Stamped from the Beginning: The Definitive History of Racist Ideas in America* by Dr. Ibram X. Kendi for a good understanding of the intersection of race and privilege.

For a quick eye opener, do a search on the internet to find out when African Americans got the right to vote. You will see information about the Fifteenth Amendment being ratified in 1870. Did you know that the Amendment did not include African American women? This simple exercise demonstrates the systemic nature of bias in the United States. A simple internet search reflects bias. The rights of men are seen as the default, even within a group of people that have experienced a long history of oppression.

African American women have three histories in the United States; some shared and one distinct. One is that which they share with African American men, one with other women, and the one that is unique to African American women. This simple example highlights the complicated history of race, gender, and intersectionality in the United States, and I have not even touched on the experience of other races, ethnicities, persons with disabilities, or the LGBTQ+ community. How could you possibly understand, change, or address all of that with a one hour, mandatory, one-size-fits-all training?

DE&I Training as a Response to an Episode

Generally, the call for diversity training happens after an episode of discrimination that becomes known. It could happen inside the company or in the community, or it could be a national high-profile incident.

Consider any of the recent events in which a customer at a major retail store was wrongly discriminated against or rudely asked to leave, based on the color of their skin. This happens more and more often, and these companies need to be seen doing something about it. They need to reassure their customers and stockholders that all is well in terms of diversity and that these were one-time episodes. That's the narrative they need to sell. Therefore, a one-time training is equal to the problem and can be seen as the fix.

If what took place is framed as an isolated incident, then all that is required of the company is a one-time training to convince everyone that the issue has been addressed and everyone can move on. There have been quite a few studies and articles to show that mandatory one-time DE&I training doesn't work because the problem we are trying to fix is not an isolated one-time event or episode. These incidents are a product of a series of connected events. They are systemic and complicated, so a complex, thoughtful, and meaningful approach is warranted.

For example, if we teach calculus in college, we make you go to class five days a week over a number of weeks because it's a complicated subject; you need repetition, and the content builds on itself. Diversity training requires the same type of approach. You must provide repetition and a chance to process and learn. It needs to be ongoing.

Also, if you are only doing one training session, the timeline doesn't always match up. Sometimes what happens is that the company trains you on bias in December, everyone takes the training, but your first hire doesn't even happen until May. By then, you've already forgotten what your biases were and what the training might have been, so it's too late. December is not when you need the training. You need it before you make a hiring decision in May.

The other reason diversity training fails, which I've already alluded to, is that your assumption about how it can potentially change your organization is well beyond what can actually happen in a one-hour DE&I training. I always tell people, "In sixty minutes, I can't make you racist. Nor can I undo racism." So, do not put that kind of expectation on a one-time mandatory diversity training. If it took someone forty-five years to develop their bias, it takes time to change them. DE&I training is just one portion of an ongoing journey that you will commit to individually and as an organization.

JASON-ISM
I can't make you racist in 60 minutes, so don't expect me to undo racism in a 60-minute training.

DE&I Training as a Series of Ongoing Trainings

The best solution is to do *ongoing* DE&I training that is provided at regular intervals, is available to every employee, and is not mandatory. Solutions typically look like the problem. You cannot get a degree in accounting in a one-hour session because there are several concepts you need to master. Additionally, many professions require ongoing certification to maintain licensure because the assumption is you have to stay current. Racism, sexism, privilege, and discrimination have a long history in the United States, and our understanding of these concepts has evolved. The protest and civil unrest of 2020 due to Breonna Taylor, George Floyd, Ahmaud Arbery, and others have reminded us that being "color blind" is not a solution, and there is still much work to be done. It will take more than a one-hour DE&I training to create understanding and effect change. These high-profile events, or events that have happened in your own company or town, are part of a series of connected events, not isolated episodes.

By establishing ongoing trainings, a more complicated understanding of our DE&I challenges can be explained, and longer-term solutions can be proposed and applied. Additionally, ongoing training signals to all employees that the DE&I program is an ongoing part of a long-term organizational commitment to cultural change. It is proof that the organization has decided to move in a direction that is about diversity, equity, and inclusion. These monthly training sessions are a reminder of that long-term commitment. This is how diversity training can be most effective.

CAPE and DE&I Trainings

Combining an understanding of the episodic versus series training approaches with the CAPE program, companies can maximize their DE&I initiatives. With CAPE, you collect data and analyze the data to find patterns. Those patterns reflect the kinds of biases (whether conscious or unconscious) an individual and or department has, so the training can be focused on those specific areas of need. Therefore, if the CAPE process identified gender bias in the marketing department, the training that marketing needs will be around that type of bias. The CAPE process will give a company the data on what the department looked like when the program started and will help document the impact of the ongoing training.

The CAPE program works in this example because:

- It started with collecting the data.
- The analysis identified a pattern.

- The plan was to reduce bias in the marketing department in the selection process (recruitment) and lower turnover (retention).
- The plan was executed with appropriate targeted training, including data to show why you are using the training:
- The plan includes the point in time the training started, how much the company invested, and the measurable outcomes that were achieved.

The Two Types of DE&I Trainings

The truth is that companies need two types of DE&I training: the broad ongoing training as well as targeted training. These work in tandem. A monthly (not mandatory) training signals to the organization that the company culture is changing. The ongoing training offered at regular intervals also allows for a deeper, more complicated conversation about DE&I. The targeted training can address unconscious bias in hiring and specific challenges reflected in the data analysis. Fundamentally, all of us see ourselves as good people, so without some targeted training to uncover our deeply held beliefs, there is no reason to change our behavior. These should be coupled together because biases and stereotypes are hard to break, so your new understanding will need repetition to create the desired long-term change. The CAPE process will help identify the content for both types of training and maximize the DE&I efforts with measurable outcomes.

Unconscious Bias

Many companies offer unconscious bias training, although many times it is not well defined. Unconscious bias is also known as implicit bias. Unlike explicit bias that reflects the beliefs or attitudes that one endorses on a conscious level, unconscious bias is the bias in judgement or behavior that results from subtle cognitive processes. Things like stereotypes often operate at a level below conscious awareness, impacting your choices and decisions about others. For example, if I were to see a monster truck, I might assume things about the person who drives it. One assumption I might make is that they don't like Black people. I have this stereotype based on absolutely no personal knowledge on my part since I've never attended a monster truck rally. Or, the second assumption would be that they listen to country music, and I also stereotype country music fans as unwelcoming to People of Color. These assumptions would impact how I think about the driver of the monster truck and if I would associate myself with them or even hire them. Most of the time, I don't think about these assumptions on a conscious level; I just assume them to be true. Think about how many times we use words like *fit* to make a decision about our next hire? We never have to define what we mean by *fit*, but everyone knows what is implied. I would not say let's not hire them because they came to the interview in a monster truck, I would say "they are not good fit" for our organization. This simple phrase is all that is needed to discriminate based on an unconscious bias.

We are bombarded with millions of pieces of information all day long, and in many cases we use our biases to organize that information quickly. Additionally, many of our friends have the same biases, so you never think about questioning your decisions or behavior. The challenge of unconscious bias is also that we don't think about it because it makes us uncomfortable. Take a moment and think about safety – how do you know when you are in an unsafe neighborhood? Do you think it is unsafe because you are seeing or experiencing actual violence or behaviors? Or, is it the color of the skin of the people that live there? What are the visual cues that you use to decide whether something is unsafe? I would imagine for many, the truthful answer would make you uncomfortable.

So, colleagues, supervisors, executives, and human resources staff, the first thing you need to do is discover your unconscious biases. But how do you do that?

First, realize you have a culture, and where there is culture, there are biases. For example, we tend to be US-centric in how we view the workplace. This means that you view the world from this particular perspective, which may or may not hold when you are working with groups outside of the United States. We also tend to have an unconscious bias against people with disabilities. We expect, for example, when we give a presentation that the audience will be able to see and hear.

There are tests that you can take to find out your own biases. One that I recommend is the Harvard Implicit Bias Test.[1] It is a good instrument, and the results can be surprising.

When I took the test, for example, I found out that I have a bias against Black people, and I am Black! How is that possible? I have worked in DE&I for over 25 years, I have done bias training. (I am actually bi-racial but most people assume I am African American.) But that is why it's called unconscious bias. You have to assume most people don't try to discriminate, but what happens in situations like mine is that your mind takes an unconscious bias shortcut, many times to avoid discomfort.

My bias actually makes sense, and it is also shared by many Black/African Americans. Why? Because we all consume the same media. If my white peers are getting negative messages about Blacks, so am I. Everyone in the United States typically consumes very similar images on social media or television. Therefore, we should not be surprised that many underrepresented groups also unconsciously internalize negative stereotypes about themselves.

One way to overcome our unconscious bias is to know you have them. The data show if you review these biases before making a decision, you are less apt to act on them. If you think about what biases you have, you may decide it's not the kind of person you want to be. It is important to make the unconscious, conscious.

The ADKAR Model

As you may recall, I introduced the ADKAR model in Chapter 2. At the end of the day, DE&I programs are about organizational change. You don't need to be an expert on ADKAR, but it can help you get the organizational change you need for a successful DE&I program. Let me explain in more detail how the ADKAR model works for DE&I programs.

Awareness

The first step in organization change is awareness. Awareness, is the A in ADKAR. Employees need to know that the organization has made a change and what will be expected of them. Both targeted DE&I training and regularly monthly trainings help employees understand what they need to do. When diversity training is done monthly, it is a constant reminder that DE&I is important to the organization. Therefore, regularly scheduled DE&I training creates awareness for everyone that it is important, whereas targeted training can help individuals in a particular department understand a challenge that may be unique to them.

Ongoing regular DE&I training is effective even if employees don't attend, as everyone still gets the message that DE&I is important to the organization because it is done with repetition. Remember, DE&I training is about awareness and content. Regular, established training is also more consistent with how people learn difficult concepts like unconscious bias, privilege, anti-racism, and so on.

Desire

The next step in the ADKAR model is desire. Employees need to have the desire to make the change. How do you create a desire within employees to align themselves with the change the organization is making? This can be a little more complicated in the context of DE&I because some may argue that not everyone cares about DE&I, and some people never will participate. This is exactly why mandatory training has not worked, but consistent and ongoing training will have impact. A one-time mandatory training puts the emphasis on attending, not learning the content. Additionally, it sends a message that DE&I was a one-time event, and we addressed it with a one-time training. As a result, your attendance is all that was required.

Ongoing and consistent DE&I training sends the message that the organization is changing and is committed to DE&I. Regular training sends the message that DE&I is core to the organization because everything the organization does that is important and fundamental is done with repetition. Employees will realize that to be successful within the organization, they must align themselves with the vision and goals of the organization, thus creating the desire needed for organizational change.

Knowledge

Once you have established awareness and desire, employees need the knowledge, the K in ADKAR. They need to know how to make the change and what is expected of them. Regular DE&I train-ings create an opportunity for employees to get the knowledge. I recommend that you establish training monthly, and it should not be required that employees attend the trainings. Additionally, the training should not require them to attend in any particular order because you do not want to create a situation where if employees miss a training, they stop coming. It is also okay to be redundant. The reality is that unconscious bias, micro aggression, gender, race, ethnicity, and so forth are complicated concepts that require repe-tition to understand, just like calculus.

Ability

After knowledge, employees need the ability, the second A in ADKAR, to demonstrate the necessary skills to make the change. We need employees to apply the knowledge. It is one thing to watch golf, but do you have the ability to play the game? DE&I pro-grams work to address things like how to reduce bias in the hiring process, create inclusive workplaces, understand other cultures, and have what can be uncomfortable conversations. To do these things, employees need the tools and opportunities to practice. The ongoing DE&I training helps build the skills and ability to use the knowledge when making hiring decisions and/or engaging in everyday interactions among employees.

Repetition

Repetition is how you get reinforcement, the R in ADKAR. Everything a company does that is important is done with repetition. Amazon sells products, McDonalds sells hamburgers, and Verizon provides mo-bile phones and cell service. These things are done with repetition so everyone in these companies knows what is important. Remember, it is okay to be repetitive in the DE&I training.

Additionally, you can get leadership buy-in by having them com-mit to attending and encouraging attendance. Leaders often ask what they can do to support the DE&I program, and Figure 13.1 gives them actionable suggestions.

What Leaders Can Do to Support DE&I	
Active DE&I Leader Expectations	Description
Be visible at DE&I events	A leader's presence at DE&I events, workshops and trainings is one of the easiest ways to show support.
Engage with employees outside of public forums	Leaders should have conversations with their team members in small groups and one-on-one interactions.
Encourage attendance at DE&I events and model inclusive behavior	Send personal reminders about DE&I events and create opportunities for employees to provide feedback.
Actively embrace the change	Apply the learnings and model the behaviors. It is OK to make mistakes. Stay in the uncomfortable space. Be transparent and show that you too are learning.
Be the A in ADKAR (Awareness)	Communicate directly with employees why the change is happening and how to align with the change. Repeat the messages via a variety of communication channels.

Figure 13.1 DE&I Leader Expectations.

I have made an adaptation to the ADKAR model to apply to DE&I, and I believe it should be seen as a continuum as opposed to a linear model in Figure 13.2. This adaptation is necessary because DE&I is broad and complicated, and it requires lots of repetition. For example, I could have a very good understanding of race, but that would not mean I also have an equally good understanding of anything to do with persons with disabilities. Moreover, even within the concept of race, an understanding of the experience of African Americans would not mean I have an understanding of the experience of a Latinx person. Each of the concepts would require an ADKAR model to increase understanding.

ADKAR FOR DE&I ORGANIZATIONAL CHANGE

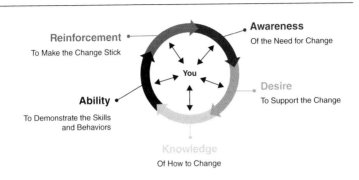

Figure 13.2 ADKAR for DE&I Organizational Change.

We need to train toward a series, not an episode – and it is going to take time. Remember, DE&I training is part of an ongoing program to move a culture; it is not a fix in and of itself. We must begin doing DE&I training as a response to an ongoing series of connected events and not as a response to unconnected episodes or events.

Key Points

- Solutions to systemic discrimination have to look like the problem – not one-time training.
- Companies need both targeted and ongoing DE&I training.
- DE&I programs are most successful when based on an organizational change model like ADKAR.
- To reduce unconscious bias, you have to know what biases you have internalized.

Note

1. The Harvard Implicit Association Test is led by Project Implicit. The test can be accessed at https://implicit.harvard.edu/implicit/takeatest.html and offers test options to assess your implicit associations in any of the following areas: Arab-Muslim, Religion, Presidents, Weapons, Age, Transgender, Sexuality, Skin-tone, Asian, Race, Weight, Disability, Gender-Science, and Gender-Career. Each test takes about 10 minutes to complete, and you are given the results and information about what it means.

Chapter 14

Inclusion Practices

Don't Ask Me to Organize the Davids

In the process of meeting new people and becoming familiar with coworkers at a previous employer, I met Dave. Dave told me, "Remember I am the only Dave. There are two or more Davids, but I am the only Dave."

Wherever you work, everyone seems to know there are several Davids but one Dave. Why is this important? It isn't, unless your name is Dave (or David). This seems complicated when I write it out, but I have found that everyone knows the Davids from the Daves. Everyone has memorized who goes by David and who goes by Dave. I have found they also know Steve from Steven, or Beth from Liz. In fact, I realized that for my entire life, in every workplace or school, people will remember who prefers to be called David or Dave. If you happen to refer to Suzy as Suzanne, she will remind you that her name is Suzy – and generally no one is offended. Most importantly, no one wants a rule that every David go by Dave. It goes without saying that asking every David in the world to go by Dave would be ridiculous.

Over my years working in diversity, equity, and inclusion (DE&I), I have found that people often want a rule. They want to know: "What are the right words to say?" or "What can I say?" They want it to be simple.

Is it Black or African American? Is it Latino or Latinx? For years I have tried to answer this question: "What are the DE&I rules?" or "What can I say and not offend anyone?" I have colleagues who have written handbooks and developed websites to help people choose the right word. Finally, I feel like I have the right answer: There are two Davids and only one Dave.

The point is: Life is complicated.

> **JASON-ISM**
>
> There are two Davids and only one Dave. That is a reminder that, just as people have preferences for different things, diversity is complicated.

All of us have many friends, family members, and colleagues, and somehow we remember all their names. If they have a unique way of pronouncing their name, we figure it out. We realize that it would be ridiculous to ask all the Davids and Daves in the world to get together, hold a conference, and decide on Dave or David.

We don't tell the world we are too busy to learn everyone's name or that it is just too complicated. Even if there is that one Dave who always gets upset if we call him David and not Dave – we respect everyone's uniqueness and realize sometimes we will get it wrong. Issues around sexual orientation, ability, gender, gender identity, ethnicity, or race are no different. It is ridiculous to think that every Latinx, LGBTQ+, or person with a disability should agree on the same term or ideology. Life is complicated.

> **JASON-ISM**
>
> Not all People of Color, persons with disabilities, LGBTQ+ individuals, or people with other identities have the same problems, issues, or opportunities. We are not a monolith.

There is a profound beauty in knowing that people can find the time to remember the Davids from the Daves. We can respect some-one's individuality. All people have a right to be who they are and what they call themselves. It is my sincere hope that as a people, we can work together on remembering what our friends and colleagues call themselves and how they like to be identified.

How to Measure Inclusion

Inclusion is one of the most difficult things to measure for any DE&I program. Inclusion is about how we treat each other. It is the words we use and the behaviors with which we interact with each other. It means we remember who goes by Dave and who goes by David. Inclusion is realizing some people prefer Hispanic or Latinx, and just because a person is from a particular ethnic group, it doesn't mean they should be required to represent and speak for the entire community.

Everyone can generally agree with the above paragraph, but how do you measure inclusion? Many have used surveys and/or pulse sur-veys. As I discussed earlier in Chapter 2, surveys are fundamentally flawed in measuring inclusion for underrepresented groups. As a quick refresher, here is a reminder of what I'm talking about – a shortened version of how surveys are flawed.

Generally, surveys are not great for measuring inclusion for three primary reasons: majority rule, anonymity, and trust. First, surveys are interpreted based on majority rule, so by definition, underrepresented groups are not a majority. So, if that group only makes up 15% of a department or company, then their responses will not have a measur-able impact on the overall score. Second, it is generally impossible for an individual's responses to be completely anonymous. If you are the only woman in the department and respond to the survey that the department leader is sexist, it will be immediately apparent who made that comment. Third, the employees have to trust the company that there will be no retribution if they are honest with their responses. If there is trust and respect in the department, there is no need for the survey; one could probably speak directly with leaders. If there is no trust, then employees will not be honest in a survey because they can't trust the leaders to treat their comments and responses respectfully and without retribution.

To solve this problem, I used the CAPE technique. Years ago, while working at the University of Colorado Health Science Center, I was added to a committee, and I don't even remember the point of the committee; I just remember I hated going to the meetings. The meetings always felt demeaning to me personally, and I never felt included. I couldn't quite put my finger on what it was about those meetings, but I hated going. I began to think maybe it was just me. I thought, "Maybe I have a bad attitude, and if I were more positive about the meetings, that would help." A better attitude did not help.

While thinking about that experience, I began to think there must be something going on in this particular meeting, as I generally enjoyed the other aspects of the job. By using the CAPE technique, I worked to find data points that could be collected and analyzed for patterns. As luck would have it, this part was already done for me. For years, there has been research to show what happens to women and People of Color in most meetings when they speak. Typically, they are ignored, or someone takes their idea, or they're challenged every time they speak up. The 2019 edition of the annual Women in the Workplace report,[1] by McKinsey and LeanIn.org, found that about half of the women surveyed had experienced being interrupted or spoken over, and 38% had others take credit for their ideas. This survey included 329 companies and more than 68,000 employees.

What I needed was a way to track these behaviors as a measure of inclusion. So, I developed the CAPE Inclusion Tracker. My plan was to use the CAPE Inclusion Tracker to track behaviors that made me feel unwelcomed (e.g., being ignored or spoken over) in meetings and use the results to increase inclusion. The data can help change behavior. If the behavior is unintentional, by sharing the information with the individual, they can change their unwanted behavior because they are no longer unaware of the behavior. If the behavior is intentional, the data will hold these individuals accountable even if they don't like it. This would be another way to work with the CEO to get support in a tangible way. The CEO can let everyone know the data are reviewed, and the expectation is to have lower scores on the CAPE Inclusion Tracker over time.

How the CAPE Inclusion Tracker Works

The CAPE inclusion Tracker is based on tracking behaviors that exclude and the behaviors that include people's voices. Figure 14.1 is a list of behaviors that are unwanted and the behaviors we would like to encourage.

The CAPE Inclusion Tracker is based on a simple point system. It assigns a positive score for each positive behavior noted in a meeting (such as redirecting) and assigns a negative score for each negative behavior (such as ignoring) identified during a meeting. The total inclusion score for the CAPE Inclusion Tracker is the total of the negative behaviors minus the positive behaviors. The goal is to decrease your score to zero, but just to be clear, it is not just about obtaining a zero score. The zero score needs to be because the negative behaviors have been eliminated, not because everyone has learned to respond to negative behaviors.

This tool is easy to use during any meeting as a tangible way to measure inclusion. Ideally, all you need is a nonparticipant observer (although you can do it yourself), pen or pencil, or use the online CAPE Inclusion Tracker.

Use the CAPE Inclusion Tracker during your meetings to document how often individual members from underrepresented groups have a negative or positive interaction within the meeting. The CAPE Inclusion Tracker (Figure 14.2) will also tell you which

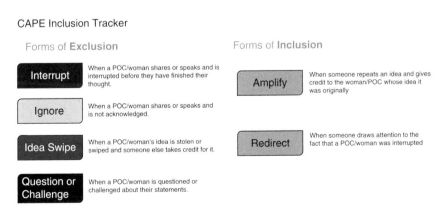

CAPE Inclusion Tracker

Forms of **Exclusion**

Interrupt — When a POC/woman shares or speaks and is interrupted before they have finished their thought.

Ignore — When a POC/woman shares or speaks and is not acknowledged.

Idea Swipe — When a POC/woman's idea is stolen or swiped and someone else takes credit for it.

Question or Challenge — When a POC/woman is questioned or challenged about their statements.

Forms of **Inclusion**

Amplify — When someone repeats an idea and gives credit to the woman/POC whose idea it was originally

Redirect — When someone draws attention to the fact that a POC/woman was interrupted

Figure 14.1 Forms of Exclusion and Inclusion.
Source: Reproduced with permission of CAPE Inclusion, Inc.

THE CAPE INCLUSION TRACKER™

GROUP	INTERRUPT	IGNORE	IDEA SWIPE	CHALLENGE	AMPLIFY OR REDIRECT	TOTAL
WOMEN OF COLOR						
MEN OF COLOR						
VETERANS						
LGBTQ+						
WHITE WOMEN						
WHITE MEN						
TOTAL						

```
                    0              2            4+
*INCLUSIVE  ◀┤───────────────┼───────────────┼─ – - EXCLUSIVE
```
*The goal is to decrease negative behavior, not to increase reactive/positive behavior.

Figure 14.2 CAPE Inclusion Tracker.

Source: Reproduced with permission of CAPE Inclusion, Inc.

underrepresented groups were most excluded. Simply mark the corresponding boxes. When the meeting is over, tally the boxes up to calculate the inclusiveness of the meeting based on your score.

The CAPE Inclusion Tracker is helpful because, to be an ally, we're told we should redirect or amplify when we observe someone's voice being ignored. So, I wanted to give an example of why redirecting can be a negative thing to see on the tracker. While it can be great that everyone is redirecting at first, if the redirecting never declines, then the underlying exclusionary behaviors have not changed. A high number of redirects means we are still seeing a lot of people being ignored, a lot of women being challenged, or a lot of women's ideas being taken from them, with someone else getting the credit. The goal is to stop the offending behavior so that redirecting is not needed. It's important to remember if you have a lot of redirecting, it is a sign that you still need to deal with those fundamental underlying behaviors. Those are what you really want to change, so the redirecting will become unnecessary.

The second piece is raising awareness about how the behavior impacts inclusion. Here's an example of what I have witnessed. While working at a previous organization, it was brought up to the CEO that every time a certain woman who was a part of the senior leadership team spoke up, people talked over her and/or they challenged everything she said. Unfortunately, the CEO did not think that was really happening, but he agreed to have a talk with her.

The CEO approached her and asked if she believed she was repeatedly spoken over or if her statements were disproportionately challenged as compared to other members of the leadership team? Her response was, "Yes, I believe that is happening," but added that she "was used to it." The CEO came to the conclusion there was no reason to change because she was used to the behavior and didn't mind. That is one of the misses I see all the time. The point is not about if an individual can take it or handle all the challenges when being interrupted or spoken over. Those behaviors are disrespectful, wrong, and not in alignment with a good company culture. Make sure that one of the things you are communicating to people is that these fundamental behaviors are wrong and need to change.

It is important that initiatives around inclusion be combined with training. In the example above, the CEO did not understand that the larger goal was to create an inclusive culture. It is not a matter of allowing behavior to continue because your employees are used to it. The goal is that employees would feel more welcome and included if the behavior stopped.

Here is why tracking behaviors that reflect bias is important:

- First, the data show whether people have bias. If they do, they are made aware of it so they can avoid letting it influence their behavior.
- Second, once you have found a way to objectively identify and count bias, you can measure the effectiveness of the training on the behavior. Remember to collect data points before and after to know that your training is actually working.

Commitment to inclusion has to be a focus for your company, and measuring inclusion has to be equally as important as supporting employees. You can do this by saying to individuals impacted by microaggressions and bias that what they are feeling is real and that you see how they are being disrespected in these meetings. You can communicate that the company is aware that people are taking credit for their ideas and people are talking over other employees. Not only should you document it via data collection, it needs to be combined with training for the employees who are responsible for the unwanted behaviors.

I have been asked if the CAPE Inclusion Tracker might be awkward in a meeting or if it can be intrusive to the flow of the conversation. My response is that it may be intrusive but not any more than being inter-rupted, spoken over, and/or having your ideas taken during a meet-ing. At the same time, I do have some appreciation for the question, and there are a couple of different ways to use the CAPE Inclusion Tracker that can be less intrusive. First, it is not unusual for meetings to be recorded and for those recordings to be made available. If there are concerns about impacting the meeting, this may be the best route. Obtain the recording after the meeting is over and have someone review the meeting and score it.

Another way to use the CAPE Inclusion Tracker is as a measure of inclusion for yourself. There doesn't have to be any announcement. I have been in meetings where sometimes I have personally felt unwel-come. I could not quite put my finger on it, but something felt off. This was a great tool for me to check my own bias. The results may validate your feelings. Alternately, the CAPE Inclusion Tracker could show that you got it wrong, and something else might be going on, but it is not bias-driven exclusion. This is a good opportunity to do some self-evaluation, as we all have biases we need to address.

The CAPE Inclusion Tracker can also be used to capture the data points that you will need to support your concerns if you choose to go to the leadership team or a manager. This will provide the basis for a constructive conversation with supporting data. It gives the manager specific behaviors that you would like to have addressed.

The Fair Pay Solution

In your DE&I work, you should make sure the *audio matches video*, and a simple way to do that is compensation. We've known for years that women and People of Color have been underpaid. As part of your DE&I commitment, from day one, make sure to just pay people equi-tably. This commitment should also be reflected in your code of con-duct, mission statement, and vision.

Compensation isn't just salary; it's all the different forms of compensation. This is a simple way to commit to a culture of equity and inclusion. People who have been paid fairly will feel more respected and are more motivated to support the company. Building a foundation around DE&I is directly tied to the work of your employees and the work you are doing to build the business. That is how you meet your goal of keeping good people working for you.

One thing people often forget is that fair compensation is something everyone who makes a hiring decision can impact. Generally, every company I have ever worked for has a pay band for every job title. Essentially, the company sets a pay range for each position title, and hiring managers are given some discretion as to the amount of salary offered to new hires or individuals receiving promotions. The recommendation from the human resources department is typically to pay in the mid-range. We could close the pay gap by simply always paying women and People of Color at the top of the pay range. This proposal may sound controversial, but the data support doing this because typically women and People of Color only apply for jobs for which they meet every requirement in the job description.[2] That would merit being paid at the top of the pay scale and also addresses historical pay inequities.

JASON-ISMS

DE&I training and programs have to be combined with policies and processes to limit people from acting on their biases.

KEY POINTS

- Respect everyone's uniqueness and realize that sometimes we will get it wrong.
- Every person of a particular identity will not agree on the same term or ideology.
- Use the CAPE Inclusion Tracker during your meetings to document how often women or individuals from underrepresented groups have a negative or positive interaction within the meeting.
- We could close the pay gap by simply always paying women and People of Color at the top of the pay range. Typically women and People of Color only apply for jobs for which they meet every requirement in the job description, which merits higher salary, and this would correct historical pay inequities.

Notes

1. Although published annually, in 2019 McKinsey and LeanIn.org partnered on a Women in the Workplace report synthesizing five years of research. Their findings fall into three overarching themes: How women are overlooked early, how women with intersectional identification face even more challenges, and how daily microaggressions continue to play out in the workforce. Accessed on April 7, 2021 at https://leanin.org/about-the-women-in-the-workplace-report#!

2. The recommendation from the People Ops department is typically to pay in the mid-range. We could close the pay gap by simply always paying women and People of Color at the top of the pay range. This proposal may sound controversial, but the data support doing this because typically women and People of Color only apply for jobs for which they meet every requirement in the job description.

Chapter 15

Your Mental Health

A Day at the Pool

Years ago, when Justus was about six, we went on a family outing to the municipal pool. The outing was pretty typical; my wife and I rounded up Justus and Piper and all the necessary gear. We had the goggles, towels, water toys, and so on.

When we got to the pool, I went to the men's locker room with Justus, and my wife took Piper to the women's locker room to put on our swimming suits. As soon as we entered the locker room, in typical fashion Justus started ripping off his clothes because he wanted to get to the pool as fast as possible. I tried to slow Justus down and reminded him we needed to find a locker to use. Too late! By this time Justus was naked and looking at me like, "Why have you not handed me my swim trunks?" Like most six-year-olds, Justus seemed oblivious to the fact that he was completely naked. Justus's only concern was getting to the pool. Apparently, I was the one that did not know how to handle himself at the pool. I quickly got Justus into his swimming trunks and rounded up the clothes that Justus has strewn all over the place. I found a locker to put our clothes in so we could get to the pool.

Justus was a very outgoing little boy and quickly made friends with anyone looking to have fun. Justus always looked out for his four-year-old sister and kept her close. We had a great time at the pool, and my wife had packed snacks and lunch. Therefore, we spent all day there, but it was still hard to get Justus and Piper out of the pool when it was time to go. It had been a long day. My wife and I were worn out, and we were ready to go home. We nicely told the kids to get out of the pool, but it was no use. As I am sure most parents can relate, by the time we got the kids to listen to us, we were on our last nerve. It took 20 minutes, but finally, the kids were out of the pool, and we were on our way to the locker room to change clothes.

I got Justus into the locker room and found our locker. I sat down for a minute to catch my breath because my nerves were a little frayed after the 20-minute ordeal to get the kids out of the pool. I got the energy to unlock the locker and dug out our towels and clothes. I was completely dressed, and I realized Justus was still in his trunks. I looked at him and said, "Justus, you need to get dressed. It is time to go." As you can imagine I was out of patience at this point. Justus just looked at me. He would not get dressed! I looked at him and said very sternly, "You need to get dressed. It is time to go!" Justus gave me this funny grin, and I realized he was now too embarrassed to get undressed and put on his clothes in the locker room. I looked at Justus and I thought, *Are kidding me?* When we got here, Justus had almost undressed in the lobby, and now he was too self-conscious.

Somehow, I found enough patience to say, "Okay, jump up here on the bench, and I will wrap you in a towel. Then you can reach under the towel and take off your trunks without anyone seeing you." Justus seemed fine with this idea and proceeded to take off his trunks while having this big towel wrapped around him just under his armpits. I handed Justus his underwear, and he started putting them on, but they got stuck somehow. He could not get the underwear past his calves. Justus looked at me as if he needed help. I said, "Just pull them up." I was tired, it was time to go, and Justus couldn't get his underwear on – how was this possible? I told Justus with what little patience I had left and through gritted teeth, "Pull up your underwear! It cannot be that difficult!" He tried, but it was no use; they were stuck. I, of course, thinking he was not trying hard enough, walked over to him and grabbed the underwear on each side and yanked. This move picked Justus right off the bench and almost put him through the ceiling. I quickly realized he was right! The underwear was stuck! How could this be happening! I pulled on the underwear again, but nothing happened. The underwear would not go past his calves. I tried to look to see what the problem was, but I could not see because Justus was wrapped in a towel up to his armpits.

I tried to pull up the towel to see better, but Justus pushed it down because he was too modest. He looked so concerned about being seen that I decided to put my head under the towel. Well, of course to do this, I had to lift the towel too high for Justus' new-found modesty. I decided, because he was standing on the bench, maybe if I knelt down I could get my head under the towel to see the problem without raising the towel too high. I now know this was not a good idea, but I was tired, and I wanted to go home.

Well, I was now completely under the towel, it was dark and hot, and the underwear was stuck to Justus because he did not dry himself off before attempting to put it on. The underwear was stuck to Justus like Super Glue. We must have looked completely ridiculous to everyone in the locker room. A little boy with a towel draped around him like a dress, and his dad under it completely covered by the towel except with my legs sticking out.

At this point, while still under the towel, I decided, I do not care what the problem is, he was going to get this underwear on! So, I just started to push the underwear up and I could hear Justus giggling. I was still completely under the towel. I couldn't see anything, but I didn't care and pushed harder. I didn't care what this looked like to anyone in the locker room. I just wanted Justus dressed so we could go home. Justus continued to giggle while I am under the towel which only annoyed me more but five minutes later, I got that underwear all the way up. I was hot, sweating, and mad at Justus for laughing at me.

I extricated myself from under the towel where it was dark and musty. I was sweating as though I had just stepped out of a steam room, and I stood up to look Justus in the eye. He was much taller because he was still standing on the bench with a funny smile on his face. I was ready to give Justus a good talking to for laughing at me and not listening to me and then – an older gentleman touched me on the shoulder. He had the most pleasant look on his face and said, "You should enjoy these days. They don't last very long." It was almost as if he would have liked to have traded places with me. It was at that moment I realized how ridiculous we must have looked. Justus and I looked at each other, and we both had a great laugh.

You know, the older gentleman was right. It is like I always say, parenting is a short season in your life, and you should make the most of it. Take a lot of trips to the pool and remember to laugh at yourself. Justus will turn 26 this year. Where did the time go? What I wouldn't give for another day at the pool!

The work of a diversity officer can be very stressful. Make sure to take time for your family, loved ones, and friends. Take trips to the pool and keep a good perspective on what really needs to get done. You won't fix racism, discrimination, homophobia, or ableism, or put in the perfect diversity, equity, and inclusion (DE&I) program in one day.

Mental Health for You and Your Colleagues

One of the biggest challenges for DE&I officers or chief diversity offi-cers (CDOs) is their own personal mental health. It is the part of the job that most people never think about when they are looking to start a career in this space. It is also the part most often forgotten after working in the space for years.

I remember years ago, I was on a panel with other diversity officers to discuss best practices for DE&I. Most of the questions were about the work, but the one question, I remember most vividly is, "What do you do to take care of yourself?"

One of the other panelists talked about all the stress they were feeling on a daily basis. This person was feeling very isolated, and although many of the DE&I initiatives were working, they were get-ting criticized by employees from all sides. The employees of Color did not feel they were doing enough to push the leadership team. The leaders did not feel they were getting enough support to change the culture, and yet they were provided no budget.

The next person was also feeling very isolated and unappreciated. (I mentioned in Chapter 11 that they cried when taking this question.) It was sad because people forget that, as a diversity officer, you have to take care of your own mental health. This has to be your priority.

There are a lot of reasons why your mental health has to be a priority. The work is difficult and can be overwhelming. People will bring a lot of problems to you, and many times you cannot fix them, or they take weeks to resolve. Equally painful is that sometimes people have racist views that they do not think are racist and are offensive to you personally. Sometimes this requires you to bite your tongue and find a way to educate them because they are trying to learn. Unfortunately, you will also find some people are just trying to be offensive and only acting as though they are trying to learn. There is no real way to separate the two, but you have to play along. This takes a lot of physical and mental energy.

Additionally, you too may be experiencing the same issues as the employees that come to you for support. In 2020, we had COVID-19, a contentious election, an economic shutdown, and heightened racial tensions. These events by themselves are very difficult to process individually, and if you are having to support others in dealing with them, they can be even more stressful. If you are not taking care of yourself, all of these things will get very, very heavy and mentally taxing.

Many times, you are trying to address and correct challenges that tend to move very slowly. The other piece of it is, many times, that you do not even have the power to make the change. So, if an employee comes to you and says, "Hey, the leadership team in this department is treating me like crap. They are being rude to me. I feel like it is racist." They come to you as if you can fix it, and many times you are not fully empowered to make that change. You cannot actually fix it. Or, if you can, you typically cannot fix it in the timeframe that is necessary for that employee. So many times, they feel like you are failing them, which of course is very hurtful for you personally.

If you never talk to anyone about these problems, or if you do not have a good peer group or support group, you are going to struggle. Your mental health has to be a priority. I would encourage you to talk to a counselor or a psychologist or someone to help you with your mental wellness. Take care of your diet, and make sure you exercise.

I remember several years ago, I went to a diversity officer conference. We had a closed-door meeting with 50 diversity officers. The person leading the conversation said, "How many of you are seeing a counselor?" Half the hands went up. Then the next question was, "How many of you want to see a counselor?" That was the other half of the room. Mental wellness should be a priority, and you have to take care of yourself. I would encourage you to make sure you have someone you talk to and do it on a regular basis.

JASON-ISMS
The one thing you can do to make a difference in DE&I? Work on yourself.

It is not something most people think about, but working on yourself is the one thing you actually have full control over. And it can make a big difference in your work and your personal life. People often ask me what is the one thing they can do to make a difference in DE&I, and my response is always to work on yourself. They are often put off by my answer, but working on yourself is the biggest difference you can make in DE&I. Running around, hoping to pull Black Folx out of fires is just not going to happen. Instead, read books and articles, watch videos, be uncomfortable, and accept that you will make mistakes.

JASON-ISMS
It is okay to cry and be angry, mad, or hurt. Discrimination is painful, and you have a right to all of those emotions.
    I have found that people get stuck. They have experienced discrimination or been hurt in some way. They don't think they should be angry or cry, but are not sure what else to do. Many times, people don't want to cry because that would show weakness or they have been told not to cry at work. Denying that emotion is not a solution as they have experienced something that is real and hurtful. It is okay to cry and be mad or hurt. We can support each other by recognizing and validating what someone is feeling.

JASON-ISMS
Do you want me to listen or fix? I can do either or both.

When employees contact me about something they are experiencing, before they get too far into sharing what has happened to them, I ask, "Do you want me to listen or fix?" Then, I let them know, "I can do either or both." I have found this simple question very helpful in framing my responses to the various situations through the years. When you get someone who is upset and bringing a problem to you, it is important to help them clarify what they want out of the conversation. If they just want an ear, someone to listen, then you can listen and validate the way they feel. This can be very helpful to an employee because many times they are in a department that has no diversity, and they need someone to validate what they may be experiencing.

If they want you to fix their problem, you will approach your listening from a perspective of action. You can also set expectations and outline the things that you can actually do. This will keep everyone on the same page and prevent people from being disappointed in your work later. One of the biggest mistakes is fixing when someone wants you to listen or listening when they want a fix.

Key Points

- Your mental health has to be a priority. I would encourage you to talk to a counselor or a psychologist or someone else to help you with your mental wellness.
- When helping employees, try to set expectations early by asking if they want you to listen or try to fix their problem.
- It is okay to cry, and be angry, mad, and or hurt. Discrimination is painful, and you have a right to all of those emotions.

Part III

Things I Wish
I Had Known

Success is not achieved by winning all the time. Real success comes when we rise after we fall. Some mountains are higher than others. Some roads steeper than the next. There are hardships and setbacks but you cannot let them stop you. Even on the steepest road you must not turn back.

—Muhammad Ali

Chapter 16

Top Challenges
for DE&I Professionals

Voices Telling You What You Can't Do

Years ago, we attended a birthday party with my son, Justus. I believe one of his friends was turning ten. This particular party was held at a local university that had a climbing wall. All the kids at the party were given a chance to try the climbing wall while one of the university's students belayed them (held the safety rope).

All of the kids attempted the climbing wall with varying degrees of success. The university students belaying the kids were very helpful and tried to direct the children to the route up the climbing wall that best suited their abilities to climb the wall. Justus was one of the last kids to get a chance to go up the climbing wall. Justus had some climbing experience and was familiar with the procedure to put on the gear and strapped everything on relatively quickly.

Justus then put on a big smile and looked at the twenty-something-year-old guy that was belaying him and said, "Which is the most difficult route up the wall?" The young man seemed a little tickled by

Justus's courage and said, "Well it is what we call *the crack*, but I would not recommend you try it. The crack is very difficult, and I can only make that route on my best days and even then, sometimes I can't make it!" This seemed like a good enough reason for me to have Justus take another route because the college student was over six feet tall and very athletic looking. The college student had also mentioned to me that he used the climbing wall every day as one of the perks of having this job. Justus looked the college student right in the eye and said, "I would like to try the crack." The young college student tried to talk Justus out of it, but Justus was adamant. The college student relented and said, "The crack starts here," and then pointed the route up the wall.

Justus looked at the wall and jumped up but no luck. He could not get a hold of anything. Justus couldn't even get started. It was clear that the crack was too difficult for a ten-year-old boy. The college student belaying Justus began to talk to him. He said, "Justus, you should try another route up the wall. The crack is very difficult, even for the best climbers." Justus took a step back from the wall and never turned around. He just stood there and looked at the wall. The college student said, "There are some other routes up the wall to your right, and they're much simpler." Justus never even turned around to look at the college student who was talking to him. He just stood, staring at the climbing wall. The college student continued to explain to Justus that the crack was too difficult and encouraged him to try something else. Justus just stood there staring at the wall, never giving any indication he was listening to the college student standing right behind him.

After watching this for several minutes, it started to get uncomfortable. The college student was talking to Justus, and Justus never looked at him. The college student continued to talk to the back of Justus's head. Other kids were waiting for their turn. Parents were getting impatient because their child was waiting for their turn. My wife nudged me and gave me a look like I should intervene and encourage Justus to take another route up the climbing wall. It started to get a little embarrassing that Justus would not even acknowledge that the college student was talking to him. Justus was just standing there staring at the climbing wall.

After a few more moments, it was clear that I had to do something. The other parents were looking even more impatient, and I could tell by the tone of the college student's voice that he was getting frustrated with Justus, especially because Justus had never given any indication he was listening to the college student. I took a step toward Justus and mumbled something. I am not sure what I said because the whole situation was awkward and uncomfortable. Justus was not typically so blatantly rude to anyone. I was a little taken back by his behavior. I took another step toward Justus and said, "Justus, you should take another route up the climbing wall."

The other parents and the college student seemed relieved that I had attempted to help get Justus's attention. Justus never even looked at me. I, too, was being ignored. Then without a word, Justus took a step toward the climbing wall and jumped. Somehow Justus had gotten a grip on the wall. Although it looked awkward, it was brilliant. Justus had jammed both hands into an opening in the climbing wall and was on his way. The college student was equally surprised but quickly gathered himself and removed the slack from the rope.

Justus conquered the crack that day, and I was the proud father. Most importantly, Justus taught me that there will always be a voice behind you telling you what you cannot do. You achieve greatness and your personal goals when you ignore the doubters and those who tell you what you cannot do.

Starting and running a DE&I program comes with challenges and many voices telling you what you cannot do. This chapter and book is dedicated to overcoming those challenges.

The Myth That Diversity Lowers Quality

This is one of the challenges you always get as a diversity officer, that when we put in some initiatives to diversify our staff, that somehow, we are lowering quality. This attitude reflects a bias in how People of Color and women are perceived, which is a great teaching opportunity. Diversity and low quality are not connected in any way. The fact is, the goal is to diversify the organization, not lower standards.

Let's imagine we begin a program to increase women in engineering because they are underrepresented. There should never be an assumption that this means we have lowered our standards. There's no connection between adding diversity and lowering standards. It's a false assumption that certain groups are underrepresented because they are destined to be failures. That false narrative relies on another false assumption: that white men never fail. The truth is that anyone can fail spectacularly – and anyone can succeed. Just think of the colossal business failures that have happened when white men were at the helm: Enron, Bernie Madoff, Blockbuster, WorldCom, Kodak, DeLorean Motor Company, Pan American World Airways, Arthur Andersen, and Lehman Brothers are just a few. But no one attributes those failures to ethnicity or gender of the people in charge.

A Hire from an Underrepresented Group Is Not Performing

One thing I often hear is, "Well, we hired a woman and she did not do well in our department, so we are not so sure about diversity." We need to separate low performance from identity. The fact of the matter is men, and particularly White men, are hired all the time, and often fail as I stated above. We do not assume failure is directly connected to their whiteness or the fact that they are White men. That again, is a misconception that has to be addressed. Men, like women, fail all the time, and just because one person fails, or you made a hire and it did not work, you should not connect that to the race or gender of every single person in that community. The real problem is the association being made between race, gender, and poor performance. We need to address that type of bias, assumption, or stereotype.

It is important that we educate people about their biases. We need to help people understand that our diversity commitment is equally about inclusion and equity and addressing assumptions that people have about quality and ability. Those things are very important and are a conversation that you need to make sure you are engaging with your employees and employer about.

Chain of Command

Who the DE&I leader reports to can be a big challenge. Generally, the best practice is to report to the CEO, and I honestly believe and encourage that, but many of you will find yourselves in the human resources (HR) department, and that can become very difficult. I know a lot of people will probably disagree with this, but I prefer not to report to HR.

One reason that reporting to HR doesn't work is that if the budget gets tight, they may say, "Well, couldn't some of the current HR staff also do some of the DE&I work?" And so your DE&I budget gets systematically reduced, and you end up with a partial staff that already has a full-time job trying to support you. It is possible that HR staff could handle some DE&I work, but the reason you were hired is that they did not have the time and/or expertise to do it in the first place. On top of that, you are responsible for DE&I tasks and have a staff that does not report to you. The problem is that if they don't do the job, you are still held accountable. Needless to say they generally do not prioritize the additional work from the DE&I program as their top priority. And I don't blame them because the additional work is typically not in their job description or measured in their yearly goals. It is extra work for which they are essentially not paid. This creates a no-win dynamic.

This happened to me several years ago. When I first started working in a particular company, I was reporting to the CEO and, due to some reorganization and budget cuts, I was reassigned to report to the senior VP of HR. When I submitted my budget request, the first response I got was, "Couldn't we save money if some of the current HR staff took on some of the DE&I work instead of hiring someone for DE&I?" I did not like the idea and voiced my concern, but the decision was made that existing HR staff would take on some DE&I work. The HR staff was already busy, and I found myself with no staff and good intentions. Everyone from HR wanted to help, but they never prioritized DE&I work because they had to meet their HR objectives first. Additionally, none of them had DE&I experience, so they needed more of my time just to get started on some projects.

Having the DE&I function report to HR also means the DE&I office has to compete on two levels for resources. First, you need to convince the HR leadership team to lobby for resources at the company level that will support DE&I. Second, you have to compete within the HR team for those resources. Even though the CEO is holding you directly responsible for diversity goals, you will find yourself negotiating directly with the HR team for resources. At the end of the day, because you report to the HR leader, they will make the decision on where those resources are allocated. As I shared in my example, you may disagree with using current HR staff in lieu of hiring, but you don't get to make the final decision. That can make it difficult to execute and or get resources in general. By contrast, if you were your own department, you could at least advocate and leverage your own funds without having another level of budget requirements for resources or staffing needs.

Your Positional Authority

Positional authority can be a challenge for DE&I because the most senior person is often a director. It is difficult for a director-level person to execute on DE&I goals. I've done it before, but I don't recommend it, mostly because you do not have enough positional authority to make changes.

Let's say the vice president of marketing is doing something, and you need them to change their behavior; you do not have enough positional authority to make that happen. That is a major challenge. Additionally, you may be two or three levels below the CEO, which may make it difficult to get on their calendar to get support to influence a senior leader. This creates a difficult dynamic for you to have any kind of influence, and, as a DE&I leader, you really need influence to do the job. If you think about it, most of the work of the diversity officer is in the realm of influencing other people because, at the end of the day, you can't make decisions about every hire in every department or how the company is marketed.

On the one hand, if you, as a director, call on others to make changes, it is much easier to dismiss you and your suggestions. I see this happen all the time. When the top DE&I officer is a director, it also speaks to the actual level of commitment within the organization. Generally, every department has a lead that is at the VP level. If your department doesn't, you probably won't have the same kind of leverage as other departments. That makes it difficult to execute your plans, especially because so many of them will involve other departments. It's not a great environment to be in, and you will typically struggle if you are at the director level.

On the other hand, if you have to call on others to make changes, and you have a VP title, it makes a difference because you have some leverage or more influence. You are seen as a senior leader, and as an executive you have positional authority.

If you don't have enough positional authority, you are not going to be successful. I've seen some companies even start with a single DE&I position at the coordinator level. Organizations that take this approach are literally setting that person up to fail because they have no positional authority. When they call people and ask them to do things, they will face resistance. Some higher-level employees will not take them seriously because a coordinator is so low on the chain of command. You've got to be able to call people and get their attention to make change because the most important thing you need when executing your plan is influence.

Staffing and Budget

Staffing and budget are always a challenge for DE&I programs. When starting a DE&I program or taking one over, be sure to ask if you will have staff or if there is a plan to add staff. This is always an ongoing challenge because companies will say, "Well, we have never had a diversity program before, so our plan is we are going to hire you and have you build the program and then develop the plan for staffing and budget."

I can tell you from experience that companies do not launch any other programs or departments without staff and budget. This only happens with diversity work. Why? Because intuitively, company leaders know if they are going to add a marketing department, the program is going to need staff and budget. If a company has 4,000 employees, it's clearly not possible for one person to handle HR, finance, sales, or any other business function without appropriate budget and staff, so how could one person support the DE&I program for the entire company? You don't need the experience of running a DE&I program to understand that one staff person would not be enough. Think of it this way, if the company adds a vice president, typically every vice president has an assistant. When you launch a DE&I program, it is important that the company fully commit to it with the staff and budget that will be necessary to execute. As I stated before, it is difficult to be successful when you are not fully supported.

I have started at many companies as the new VP of DE&I. On the first day, I am introduced to other VPs, and all of them had at minimum an administrative assistant to manage their calendar. I was almost always hired without administrative support or a plan to get support. I found myself quickly overwhelmed as scheduling meetings is one of the first things you need to do. I spent a lot of time talking to and emailing other VP's assistants to schedule meetings instead of doing the work. Generally, the solution would be to have someone else's assistant help me. I always welcomed the help, but it was the same old problem.

Generally, I find that almost every diversity program is under-funded. This means DE&I programs are not fully resourced to address the issues they have been asked to fix. Generally, what happens is that a company has 10,000 employees and one diversity officer. If you're lucky, you may have a $50,000 budget. If you think about it, there is probably no other department in the organization that has a budget so small, that is asked to support the entire organization.

As an example of the how small DE&I budgets are, over the last 20 years almost every company I have worked for has had across-the-board budget cuts. In this scenario every department has been asked to reduce their budget by 5% or some standard amount to reduce cost for the orga-nization. My budget was so small in comparison to other departments, I was generally not required to reduce my budget as it would have no impact on reducing the overall expenditures of the organization.

When it comes to a low budget or no budget at all, the CAPE process can be very helpful to you, and that is why I created it. If you collect your data, analyze it, and use that analysis to make your plan, you will be maximizing the limited resources you have in the most effective way possible. The CAPE process helps you to know what the best use of your time is and how to maximize your bandwidth and limited resources. You're not going to be able to fix everything at once. The CAPE process helps you define what is the best use of your time, prioritize, and show results.

Diversity Committees

As previously mentioned, diversity committees can be a challenge. Generally, when they exist, they think they're a decision-making body, and you find yourself competing with this committee. Sometimes they are floundering, and they want you to fix the committee. That can be difficult because often the problem is that each committee member wants the authority to make decisions, which can become a distraction and take up a lot of time.

Another thing that happens when working with a diversity committee occurs when you're launching a program or taking over an existing program. The committee may have a plan in place. In many cases, even if the diversity program has struggled, the committee is still committed to their original plan. You need to be in a situation where you can adjust their plan if necessary. The truth is that many plans are built on goals that are not achievable. Or they are so theoretical, there is no way to know whether or not you are achieving them. For example, the committee's plan will have goals like *We should be an inclusive environment.* Great. What does that mean? How do I know when the environment is inclusive if the plan includes no metrics? Inclusion is a cultural value, which means that the organization typically never gets there, but the committee continues to hold on to a goal that has not been defined.

You may also find yourself at odds with the DE&I committee because they don't have a great understanding of DE&I and want all 10,000 employees to be at a certain level of understanding of diversity, equity, and inclusion by some set date. This an unachievable goal, especially if you are the only staff person and you have a limited budget. On top of that, instead of focusing on your own data and planning, you may have to spend a lot of time bringing the committee up to speed on DE&I. They will need to understand that a successful diversity program may never get 10,000 employees to the same understanding of DE&I. You need to have the power to change the plan, if one exists. Everyone wants a successful DE&I program, but not everyone knows how to implement a successful DE&I program.

Working with Other Departments

Working with other departments is one of the biggest challenges for diversity programs. For example, you don't actually make the hiring decisions, but you are held accountable for the diversity of the organization and each department in it. It is challenging when you have goals for other departments for DE&I to execute because you're not the final decision maker on hiring or other day-to-day decisions.

Additionally, items like website updates, new products, or more diverse marketing outreach can all be good ideas, but you aren't directly involved in those efforts. For example, you don't choose when website changes will be made. You might think, "Our website should reflect more diversity." Great. At the end of the day, you don't make that decision or when it will be implemented. That is made somewhere else, usually in marketing or communications. So it's important to understand the challenges of a diversity officer when working with other departments. Most of the power you have is influence, which is why you need to have a VP title rather than a director title.

I remember years ago, when I worked at a company that had outdated DE&I information on their website. There was a reference to a DE&I commitment the company had made to the Obama administration. Unfortunately, at that time, Obama had not been in office for over a year. It took another year for me to get the IT team to remove the reference. It was not something in my direct control, although people would ask me about the reference on the website because it was DE&I related. I would be in meetings and at events, and people would ask me about the DE&I commitment. It became embarrassing to the company, yet I could not get the IT team to remove the reference. The IT team would tell me they were planning on changing it as part of a larger website rebuild, so they had it on their list of things to be done. Again, my priority was not their priority.

Efficacy of Résumé Redacting

Résumé redacting does not work and reinforces bias. Résumé redacting is the process of removing things that may indicate a person's race, ethnicity, gender, or other parts of their identity from the résumés. The reason it doesn't work is that bias does not live in the résumé. It lives in the people making the decision and reviewing résumés. That is who and what has to be addressed. You can do the résumé redacting, but at the end of the day, generally the hiring will be made on an in-person interview. For example, if a hiring manager has a bias against women, all it does is make that bias come into play at a later point in the interview process. So typically, when a person has gender bias, it would first be evident when résumés are being reviewed. When résumé redacting happens, the hiring manager can't remove women from consideration during the résumé review period. Instead, they will remove women from consideration when the candidates come in for the interview. Because we've never addressed the underlying bias, it's going to keep happening. The applicant's Hispanic surname, gender, or other references to their identity in the résumé is not the problem. The hiring manager is the problem, and you need to address that issue directly. Résumé redacting only changes the point in time when the discrimination takes place; it doesn't eliminate it from the hiring process. Use the CAPE process to identify where in the organization you have hiring bias. Then provide those individuals with training and use the data to hold them accountable. This is also where to get CEO commitment. The CEO should review hiring patterns on a regular basis with leaders.

Belonging versus Inclusion

I have spent too much time trying to explain the difference between belonging and inclusion. Worrying about terms like *belonging* is a distraction that wastes your time and focus. Don't create too many terms. Diversity, equity, and inclusion are enough. When I first started, they called it minority affairs. It progressed to multicultural affairs, diversity, diversity and inclusion, and now diversity, equity, and inclusion. No matter the name, I've done the same work for 25 years. Now we call it diversity, equity, and inclusion (or sometimes diversity, equity, and belonging). Don't overthink it.

The reason I don't like *belonging*, in particular, is that it is hard to separate belonging from inclusion, and you find yourself in long conversations trying to separate the two. Even if you can, it's still not a great definition and not worth the time. Belonging sounds great, but I don't belong to you and, generally, employees don't belong to their organizations. The word has an inherent connotation of ownership or obligation, which in my mind, is fundamentally wrong.

Many of us have heard the dancing analogy that being invited to the dance is one thing but being invited to actually dance is belonging.

Just because you dim the lights and turn on the music doesn't mean I have to dance with you. Everyone can say, "No, I don't want to dance with you." That's my right, too, and that should be respected. There should be no retribution for not dancing with you or the assumption that I should be dancing with you. I also want to validate that some could not get to the dance, and we should also concern ourselves with what are the barriers to getting to the dance. What does that mean in the real workplace? To me, this issue is connected to equity, which is how we treat people. Belonging strikes me as a violation of equity. I'll explain what I mean using two examples.

First, bonuses are often based on employees doing "above and beyond" what is required for their jobs, "above and beyond" is not clearly defined. This means it's often totally subjective, and the only way to know how get the bonus is if you're part of the *in-group*. The *in-group*, the people who really *belong*, get the message about what constitutes "above and beyond." Whereas employees who are outside of the *in-group* often don't get that coded information. In this sense, *belonging* is a code word, similar to *fit* (see Chapter 9).

The second example of how the idea of belonging can undermine equity comes into play when the definition of "above and beyond" is made clear to everyone. Suppose, going "above and beyond" is all about coming in early and staying late. Suppose a single parent interviews for a position where this is the unspoken policy. HR and the hiring manager aren't likely to say, "The official hours are 9 to 5, but to qualify for the bonus, you need to work 7 to 7." They probably said, "The salary is X, and there's an opportunity for a bonus for "above and beyond" performance." Not everyone can work extended hours, and this criterion disproportionately impacts women with children. As a result, the bonus plan systematically punishes women because it penalizes anyone with child care obligations who may not be able to work extended hours.

Rules, compensation, and processes shouldn't be about whether or not you *belong* in the group, meaning you can decipher the code words (e.g., "above and beyond") and meet the unspecified extra requirements. Work should be equitable. Everyone should have the same access to information and have the same opportunities. I should not have to "belong" to the in-group to get a bonus or other opportunities for promotions.

Allies

In my mind, people who describe themselves as *allies* need to under-stand that the first step is to humble themselves and listen. The challenge with allies is that many times people come with the attitude that they are there to save someone. That mentality creates a power dynamic where the ally thinks, "I have this power, and I use it to help you." Instead, allies should think, "We are peers, and I use my power to respect you." To truly be an ally, you must respect me and my experi-ence and act that way when I'm not in the room. If your assumption is you're my ally, and you're here to help me, the only time you're going to help me is if you think I'm struggling. I need you to speak up when I'm not in the room. That's fundamentally what needs to happen, and what allies have to do.

Making the Implicit Explicit

If we want to have an equitable environment, we need to look at the systems and processes to uncover the patterns. If you look around the department and realize that everyone knew the department head from a previous job or went to college together, that tells you something about the hiring process. You have some implicit rules that make it impossible for someone outside of your network to get a job at your company.

DE&I programs need to create networking opportunities, not men-torship or developmental programs. I have found that "developmental" programs for People of Color or women send the signal that they are not ready for leadership opportunities. Their White male peers do not need these programs for leadership positions, but somehow women and People of Color need such programs to be ready. The implicit message of leadership development or mentorship programs is that participants are not ready to lead. Therefore, how a program is positioned is equally important as the content. At the end of the day, the reason my White peers received promotions is partly because of their networks. Learning from this, DE&I programs need to create inclusive networks to foster opportunities for meaningful interaction between leaders and under-represented groups.

> **JASON-ISM**
> What do DE&I programs do? They move processes like "how to network" from implicit to explicit.

You need to make everything explicit and review those processes for bias. One of the things DE&I–related initiatives do is make implicit process explicit. Equity can only exist when all the rules about hiring, compensation, and promotions are explicit and shared with everyone.

Bridging the Gap Between Intent and Impact

In order to build a dynamic company, you have to understand what will be going on in the future and plan for that change. The question I have for you is: What kind of company are you building? Are you building *today's* best company or *tomorrow's* best company? DE&I has to be a part of that vision.

> **JASON-ISM**
> DE&I has to be aligned with the larger mission and vision of the organization.
>   Aligning your DE&I program with the mission and vision of the company and its definition of diversity within the context of the company allows you to construct a program that is most likely to make an impact for that organization. Never take a one-size-fits-all approach with your DE&I program.

Due to all of the social activism of 2020, many companies made statements about their commitment to diversity, equity, and inclusion. Those statements will not be enough. Companies will need to bridge the gap between what they say and what they do. Both internal and external stakeholders will be looking for this alignment between audio and video. The question of whether you are building today's best company or tomorrow's best company is especially important in DE&I. Many DE&I programs need a long-term strategy to fully imple- ment solutions, specifically, those that relate to hiring, promotions, board and leadership diversity. Because you are working toward a longer time frame, you need to be building *tomorrow's* best company from a DE&I perspective.

Having diversity, equity, and inclusion woven into your goals helps you understand how DE&I connects to employees and the company. One of the common questions often asked is, what is the ROI on diversity, and why should we do this? Here are some reasons:

- Diverse companies have 90% higher retention.
- Gender-diverse companies typically perform better.
- Racially and ethnically diverse companies perform better.

Most importantly integrating DE&I with larger organizational initiatives will hold the company accountable for their public commitments.

Validating the Experiences of Others

I always tell people that listening is a key skill for a diversity officer. Many times, people will say, "Oh, so-and-so always complains." In many instances, what they need you to do is validate their experience. Suppose there are only a few People of Color or a few women in an organization. One of them comes to you and says, "I feel like people treat me poorly here, but I can't put my finger on it." If you respond by saying, "Oh, it's probably nothing. I don't think they mean it that way," you're actually going to make the situation worse.

Think of it like the movie *The Truman Show*. Truman became concerned because he kept noticing something was wrong in the world, but everyone kept telling him, "No, no. Nothing's wrong in the world." The only other resolution to that would be, "I must be losing my mind." It's the same idea with DE&I. If I tell you I'm experiencing something, but everywhere I go, people tell me it's not true, I began to question my own beliefs, existence, and reality. This has been an ongoing challenge for me when I work with employees from underrepresented groups, who many times are in an organization where they feel unwelcomed. Their reality continues to be questioned by people telling them that what they are experiencing isn't real, but they know they're experiencing it. It creates this disconnect and makes it difficult to come to work.

It's important that we validate another person's experience as real. It doesn't necessarily mean you have to agree with it, but you have to be a good listener. Listen to what is happening to them because it could be true, but also because it is a way to help a person to process, come up with solutions, and understand what might be going on. If you can help validate them, you can then support them to create the kind of environment that everyone wants, one that's diverse, inclusive, and equitable.

KEY POINTS

- Diversity and DE&I programs do not lower quality. There is no evidence that ethnicity, gender, and other elements of identity determine a person's success.
- Effective DE&I programs need staff and budget, just like any other department with a company-wide mandate.
- Positional authority is important for DE&I practitioners because their work is largely based on influence. It is difficult to influence other departments if the top-level DE&I officer is a director rather than a vice president or higher-level executive.
- Support inclusion by changing implicit processes to make them explicitly clear to all employees. This may present opportunities for you to ensure polices that used to be implicit are fair and nondiscriminatory.
- Align your DE&I efforts with the organization's larger goals, mission, vision, and strategy. That will ensure your policies will continue to fit the organization as it changes.

Chapter 17

Jason-isms

The Gift of Time

I am not much of a book reader. I don't read many books because I am dyslexic and reading takes a lot of effort.

As a kid, I was a terrible reader, and I never could sound-out words. In fact, I would often need to have the same word read to me over and over. Those who helped me, primarily my brothers, would say to me, "I just told you that word." In my mind, it was a new word every time. It then became apparent to me as a child that the only way I was going to read was to memorize what words looked like. I memorized words the way you know a stop sign. Everyone knows the shape of a stop sign without sounding out the word on it. As a result, I read every word based on what it looked like and could not spell to save my life. Having to memorize what words looked like was a very long process since I was about nine when I began doing it, and it took a lot of repetition.

One of my most vivid memories of learning to read was of my father helping me. It was on a Friday night because my dad was in a bowling league, and he always took a shower before leaving. For some reason I was attempting to read a book. This was always a challenge because my brothers would get tired of helping me. I would not use my mother because she was not really able to help me. (My mother was born and raised in Japan, and she had limited English fluency.) My two older brothers were very nice, but they would get tired of me, so I would have to limit the number of times I asked for help and go between them from room to room.

On this particular evening, I was getting very weary of going from brother to brother, and they had their fill of seeing me. I was the youngest, and it was clear they were tired of my asking for help on what I am sure seemed like every other word, and in some cases the same word over and over. I knew the only place to get help was my dad, even though he was in the shower. So I went into the bathroom and said, "Dad, can you help me?" He said, "What do you need?" I said, "I need help reading." My dad's response was what I expected, "Go ask your brothers. I am in the shower!"

Now the whole process would start over. First I asked my brother Jarred, who said "I just told you that word. Go ask Norris." Then, I went to my oldest brother, Norris, where I got a similar response, "Go ask Jarred!"

I yelled back, "I did, and he told me to ask you."

Norris said, "Go ask Dad then!" By this time, I was worn down. I thought, *Will no one help me?* So, I decided to ask my dad one last time, even though he was in the shower.

Unfortunately, by this time, little tears had started down my face. I was fighting them, but it was no use. Being in a home of three boys, I did not want anyone to see me cry, but it was too much that day. I knew I needed to learn to read, but no one would help, and I was terrible at reading. I knew I was just feeling sorry for myself, and my dad would not be very understanding.

I opened the door to the bathroom anyway and tried to collect myself. I could not let my dad know I was crying. Luckily, Dad was still in the shower, so I took a deep breath and tried to speak without sounding like I was crying. I said, "Dad, can you help me with this word?"

My dad quickly said, "I told you to go ask your brothers!"

This was actually good news because this meant he could not tell I was crying. So, I responded by saying, "I did, and they told me to ask you. They won't help me anymore." Unfortunately, when I finished the last sentence my voice cracked and my secret was out.

My father did not respond. He was in the shower, and I was in the corner crying, and he, too, would be disappointed in me. It seemed like the silence lasted forever. I looked at the shower curtain, preparing myself for his disappointment in me, when out popped my dad's face with a big smile. He said, "Let me see the word." He read it to me, popped his head back in the shower and said, "Read to me out loud." I read out loud, and if there was a word I did not know he would say, "Spell it." I would spell it out loud, and he would tell me the word. I probably only read for about five or ten more minutes, but it is one of my best memories of time spent with my father.

I hope to someday find the right combinations of words to bring as much happiness and compassion as my father gave me on that evening. I hope that everyone will be able to give the compassion and understanding that I felt on that day. Time is a simple gift and not hard to give.

Throughout my life, time has been one of the most powerful things given to me. Hopefully the time you spent reading this book will be time well spent for you. This particular story is one that gives the most insight into my life because I have always struggled to read (and write), and I still do to this day. I have dyslexia and did not know it until I was 50 years old and learned that from an NPR story.

The understanding of my dyslexia gave me pause, and I took some time to reflect. It now makes sense to me why I misspell my own name about 70% of the time. I am still not sure how I ever learned to read as I got no help in school, and education was not a priority in the home I grew up in. All together, these are the things that have shaped who I am. My dyslexia forced me to spend a lot of time working on reading and looking for patterns and shortcuts as a way to overcome my disability. Below you will find the Jason-isms. I think of these as shortcuts to help you remember some of the key ideas about DE&I and to keep perspective. Those who know me have become accustomed to hearing these and say they have been helpful. I hope the time you spend reading the Jason-isms will help you too.

The Jason-isms

- **Audio must match video.** Your verbal commitments to DE&I need to match your actions, or no one will believe or support your program.

- **Good DE&I programs are not without tension.** This is because inclusive and equitable work cultures create an environment where people can speak up and disagree without retribution. I am made more concerned when no one speaks up on contentious issues.
- **One of the biggest challenges for diversity programs is unrealistic expectations.** You can't make the board more diverse overnight, leadership teams don't become more diverse in a week, and not everyone employed will develop a high-level understanding of DE&I on the same day.
- **There are two main things that all DE&I programs do: recruitment and retention.**
- **In DE&I, it all starts with data.** If you don't know where you started, you won't know if you have made any progress. How do you fix something if you have not diagnosed the problem?
- **Do you have a recruitment problem or selection bias?** You need to know if hiring managers have section bias or they did not have any candidates from underrepresented groups to interview and hire.
- **DE&I training is not a fix in and of itself.** Getting people to change what they believe or overcome bias takes time and commitment.
- **What do DE&I programs do?** They move processes like "how to network" from implicit to explicit.
- **DE&I training is part of an ongoing program to achieve organizational change in the company culture.**
- **Your diversity program should look like your company.** If your industry or company has strict processes, the DE&I program should reflect that cultural value.
- **Whose mother are we talking about? I agree we have become way too sensitive because the jokes about your mom are really funny.**
- **The biggest challenge of DE&I programs when it comes to hiring is the concept of _fit_.** _Fit_ is a code word used in the hiring process to exclude anyone who looks different or may have a different perspective.
- **People have a right to be sensitive, protective, and to voice when they have been offended. We can all apologize and learn.**
- **Having 50% diversity on the leadership team sounds great, but you would need approximately 50% of the current leaders to leave to get to that kind of number. It is just unrealistic.**
- **ERGs can be your best friend or your worst headache. Learn to use them to lighten your load.**

- DE&I committees work for you, not the other way around.
- I can't make you racist in 60 minutes, so don't expect me to undo racism in 60 minutes.
- **There are two Davids and only one Dave.** That is a reminder that, just as people have preferences for what they call themselves, they have a right to how they identify. Diversity is complicated, and so are people.
- Not all People of Color, persons with disabilities, LGBTQ+ individuals, or people with other identities have the same problems, issues, or opportunities. We are not a monolith.
- DE&I training and programs have to be combined with policies and processes to limit people from acting on their biases.
- Diversity programs have competing interests. You can't become more diverse if you don't have turnover, and no one wants high turnover.
- **The one thing you can do to make a difference in DE&I? – Work on yourself.** Running around hoping to pull Black Folx out of fires is just not going to happen.
- **It is okay to cry and be angry, mad, or hurt.** Discrimination is painful, and you have a right to all of those emotions.
- **We must begin doing DE&I training as a response to an ongoing series of connected events and not as a response to unconnected episodes or events.** Solutions to systemic discrimination have to look like the problem – not one-time training.
- **Aligning your DE&I program with the mission and vision of the company is the first step.** Everyone needs to understand how what they do aligns with the company's commitment to diversity. Never take a one-size-fits-all approach with your DE&I program.
- **Everyone should be using the same definitions for diversity, equity, and inclusion.** Having a shared language and understanding will make it easier to agree on where the DE&I program is going.
- **You do not need to be perfect to talk about DE&I, but you have to be present.**
- **Address or fix.** When someone says something racist, sexist, or something else off color, ask yourself, "Can this be fixed in this moment?" Generally, most people or "isms" can't be fixed in that moment but will need to be addressed, not for the person who said it but for the others in the room who look to you to lead.

KEY POINTS

- Use the Jason-isms as shortcuts to help you do your DE&I work. They can help you remember key concepts and communicate them in a clear and memorable way.

Conclusion

Obama out.

—President Barack Obama, from his final White House
Correspondents' Dinner speech

"Obama out." Just thinking about these two words above puts me in a good mood, and I hope reading them did the same for you. (Most importantly, I can say I quoted President Barack Obama in my book.) Life is full of small wins. You should take every one.

This book is about the lessons I learned over a 25-year career as a diversity, equity, and inclusion practitioner. Over the last 25 years, what has changed? What have we learned? Sometimes I am not sure what has changed. In 1991, the first year into the start of my career, we did diversity training as a response to police brutality and what happened to Rodney King. Now, 25 years later, we are talking police brutality and what happened to George Floyd. I would like to think between then and now, a lesson has been learned.

If you get nothing else from this book, let it be that DE&I training cannot be done as a response to a single episode. It must be done as a response to a series of connected events. We are making systemic change.

Over the course of my career, I have realized that you should take every small win. Some DE&I programs move more slowly than others, but there are always small wins along the way. Why do DE&I programs move so slowly? Because they look like the problem we are trying to fix. Change takes time, and cultures move slowly. Hopefully the tips and CAPE process from this book will prove helpful to you.

I am a very practical person, and my goal with this book was to give you some practical advice to help you do your work. The CAPE process is about helping you know: What data to collect, how to effectively analyze and assess that data, how to use it to set the right diversity goals for your organization given your current resources, how to measure the impact of your DE&I efforts, and most importantly, how to show the success of your DE&I efforts. Take all the small wins! "Obama out!"

Acknowledgments

The artwork on the cover is from my son Justus who also happens to be dyslexic. He is not an artist, but he won an art competition in the fourth grade. (Justus graduated from college about three years ago.) My favorite memory of the art competition is that Justus's teacher was very emotional at the event because Justus thanked her for helping him. Apparently, none of her previous students had thanked her. Sometimes it is the simplest gesture that can be very powerful. This was a reminder for me to thank those who have helped me along the way.

I would like to thank Dr. Dolores Saucedo Cardona, my first mentor and the one who helped start my career with her belief in me. That gift of confidence is the seed that planted my career. I would like to thank my mom for her silent strength even when there was no reason to get back up. My brother Jarred because he sacrificed his happiness to give me happiness in a home that often did not have much hope. My big sister "Jo" because she could see a little boy that needed a big sister.

Writing a book is big task, so I want to thank Deb Eldridge for her edits and time. This book was an idea, but it needed focus, and Deb helped us find that path.

I want to thank my son and daughter, Justus and Piper. In life you get many gifts, and some of the gifts change your life. Justus and Piper have been the gifts that changed my life. They have given me perspective, laughs, memories, and the understanding of love that only comes with being a dad. I hope to someday be the person they think I am. I hope to also be worthy of the love they give to me so freely.

We wrote this book! Elizabeth, thank you. This book did not get written without you. There were many days where I could not find the strength, and you carried me. Writing this book as someone who has struggled to read and write all my life comes with many reminders of pain and insecurities. Thanks for the patience to be there when the memories hurt and shook my confidence. Thanks for staying when many of those that started this book journey fell away. Thanks for staying when there was so many broken promises and insults. Thanks for believing in me when I could not find the belief in myself. Thank you!

About the Author

JASON R. THOMPSON

Jason R. Thompson is a thought leader in Diversity, Equity, and Inclusion, having spent the past twenty-five years building DE&I programs in sports, health care, technology, and education. Jason is currently the vice president for Diversity, Equity and Inclusion (DE&I) at Western Governors University (WGU), one of the largest fully accredited online universities in the United States with over 121,000 students. Jason is also the co-founder and senior advisor to CAPE Inclusion, an innovative Diversity, Equity, and Inclusion platform to collect, analyze, plan, and execute your diversity goals.

Thompson is regularly sought out for advice and leadership on how to create, grow, measure, and sustain a DE&I program by DE&I officers across the corporate and nonprofit sectors struggling to have their DE&I efforts impact their organization. Thompson developed the initial diversity and inclusion program for the United States Olympic and Paralympic Committee and created the DE&I Scorecards to measure diversity within the US Olympic and Paralympic movement. As a result of this path-breaking innovation, the USOC became the first large sports organization in the United States to release their diversity data.

The diversity and inclusion programs Jason developed have won numerous awards at the local and international level. Most recently the DE&I Scorecard developed by Jason received the top honor in the 2016 International Innovations in Diversity Awards program from the *Profiles in Diversity Journal*. Jason was also recognized as a 2017 and 2018 Diversity Leader by the *Profiles in Diversity Journal*. In 2015, the USOC DE&I department received the Diversity Champion Award for Excellence from the Colorado SHRM.

Jason has served on local, regional, and national committees for multiple organizations, including the founding member of the Diversity and Inclusion Sports Consortium (DISC), one of the largest DE&I focused sports organizations in the United States with participation by the NBA, NFL, MLB, PGA of America and the NCAA.

Thompson earned a master's and bachelor's degrees in sociology from the University of Wyoming. Jason's work has been highlighted and quoted in *USA Today*, the *Washington Post*, CNN, the *New York Times*, and the *Guardian*.

Index

Page numbers followed by *f* refer to figures.